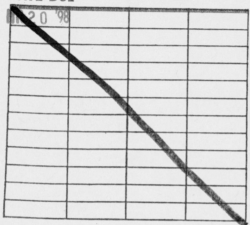

competency-based education

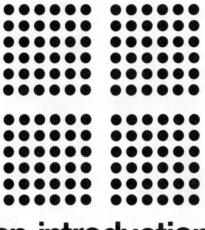

an introduction

richard w. burns and joe lars klingstedt
university of texas at el paso

editors

educational technology publications
englewood cliffs, new jersey 07632

Library of Congress Cataloging in Publication Data

Burns, Richard W   comp.
    Competency-based education.

    Articles reprinted from Educational technology,
Nov. 1972.
    1.   Individualized instruction—Addresses, essays,
lectures.   2.   Academic achievement—Addresses, essays,
lectures.   I.   Klingstedt, Joe Lars, joint comp.
II.   Title.
LB1031.B87   371.39'4   73-3133
ISBN 0-87778-061-7

Printed in the United States of America.

Library of Congress Catalog Card Number:
73-3133.

International Standard Book Number:
0-87778-061-7.

First Printing: May, 1973.

Contents

v

Contents

competency-based education
an introduction

1

Introduction to
Competency-Based Education

Richard W. Burns and Joe Lars Klingstedt

The collection of eighteen chapters represents, to our knowledge, the first effort to present an authoritative treatment of major aspects and issues relating to competency-based education (CBE) in a single source. Although most of the literature related to CBE is concerned with teacher education, this book correctly deals with CBE as a general concept applicable to all levels of learning.

Even though many authorities do not distinguish between the terms "performance-based education" and "competency-based education," there have been distinctions made, as explained in the first chapter by Klingstedt and in the chapter dealing with achievement testing by Burns.

The chapters in this book are authored by educators who have gained recognition in the field of CBE: they were invited to contribute manuscripts on this basis. Each author is expressing his or her own views and reactions to CBE. Because of this fact, and because the authors did not have an opportunity to "compare notes," a number of points of view are represented in the treatment of the various topics. The sequence of chapters moves from basic theoretical assumptions and justifications to practical applications to results of implementations.

The following chapter identifies the philosophy of education (Experimentalism) from which CBE evolved. In addition, exam-

Richard W. Burns is Professor of Education and Joe Lars Klingstedt is Assistant Professor of Curriculum and Instruction at the University of Texas at El Paso.

ples are given which illustrate some ways in which ideas in CBE might be utilized from a different point of view (Process Structuralism).

Psychological implications of CBE are treated in the next two chapters. The first, authored by Young and Van Mondfrans, compares CBE and traditional systems of instruction from a psychological frame of reference. It offers a clear explanation of, as well as a cogent argument supporting, CBE. Next, Kidd and Natalicio continue the psychological treatment with an in-depth analysis of CBE from a process or systems viewpoint. They show how behavioral analysis of a learning system can produce flexible behavioral outputs in contrast to rigid behavioral forms.

In "A Search for New Direction in Canadian Teacher Education," Halamandaris and Loughton build a case for teachers trained in "empathy-competence." They propose the use of observational techniques to identify this special aspect of teaching performance. The concept is intriguing and shows promise, if instructional methods (not presented) can be identified which will effectively promote the accomplishment of this goal.

Basic to any CBE program is the means whereby competencies are identified and defined. Burns, in the chapter entitled "Behavioral Objectives for Competency-Based Education," explains the role of behavioral objectives in defining the nature of and minimum expectancies for learned behaviors as well as the role of experience objectives in any system of learning. In the next chapter, Harbeck explains the difficult role of developing attitudes, interests and appreciations (affective behaviors) in competency-based learning. She points out the frustrations and the progress being made in attempts to provide for affective, as well as cognitive and psychomotor, learning outcomes.

The eighth and ninth chapters deal with instructional approaches within CBE. The chapter by Klingstedt, dealing with learning modules, explains the rationale for and structure of these learning packages. Burke, O'Neill and Welsch treat the use of computers in a system of humanized instructional management.

In the next two chapters, Ellis and Aubertine present guidelines for developing competency curricula at the elementary and secondary levels. Ellis relates the problem of designing elementary school curricula to the problem of adequate teacher preparation. He also lists the factors he believes will be influential in shaping future elementary curricula, and pointedly describes some of the associated problems which must be faced in implementing a competency-based curricular design. At the secondary curriculum level, Aubertine stresses the need for "relating disciplines," the development of "logical thinking," and the effective use of "language."

Achievement testing, as it relates to competency-based education, is in dire need of being rethought and restructured from a norm-referenced basis to a criterion-referenced approach. Criterion-referenced tests are new and generally misunderstood. Burns presents a thorough analysis and description of the need for criterion-referenced tests, what they are, and how they can be utilized in competency education.

In his chapter, "Certification Issues in Competency-Based Teacher Education," Andrews points out that competency-based teacher education and competency-based certification are two different concepts which involve many separate issues. He calls for a new certification system based on specific objective criteria used as standards of measurement. He concludes by predicting that all fifty states will soon be moving in the direction of competency-based education and competency-based certification. In the next chapter, Gay and Daniel explore the accreditation problems which have come full circle with the trend toward performance-based teacher education. They believe any new problems and progress toward their solution can be met effectively by present technology if society in general and educators in particular desire to meet the problems directly and work cooperatively together toward their solution.

The last four chapters deal with special issues related to the implementation of CBE. Wall and Williams present a model of how communications technology can be related to CBE. They show how technology can be utilized to implement two basic educational features (providing information and training and certifying the quality of student performance) typically within the province of schools. Additionally, they pursue conditions and problems which must be faced if any technology-based evaluation of our school system is to become a reality. Alschuler and Ivey cover the human side of CBE, which deals with those issues relating to ethical, moral, motivational and human relations skills. Another issue of CBE is how to relate it to other recognized trends, such as the utilization of open classrooms. Rice explains how the open classroom can utilize flexible strategies to develop both cognitive and affective goals, specified as competencies, whether such goals are set by teachers or learners. Lessinger explores the implications of CBE for urban children. He indicates that the main implication of CBE for urban children is its revision of traditional thinking about aptitude. He points out that CBE does not ignore the fact that students differ in their aptitude for learning. Rather, it presents aptitude as a function of the amount of time and resources needed to attain an operational description of competence instead of mastery attained in a given program in a given time. An educational system emphasizing competency would insure that each individual obtained what was necessary to function effectively in society. This, Lessinger points out, would be good news for our urban children.

A special concluding annotated bibliography reviewing the research of CBE as it relates to teacher education has been compiled by Burdin and Mathieson. It appropriately summarizes the one area of learning, teacher preparation, which to date has received the greatest attention in attempting to relate specified performances to viable learning programs. If CBE is to be extended to other educational areas and levels, the first need will be for CBE-trained teachers.

2

Philosophical Basis for Competency-Based Education

Joe Lars Klingstedt

Competency-based education (CBE) is founded on educational justifications derived from the philosophy of education known as Experimentalism. While this is true, it does not mean that one must be an Experimentalist to utilize ideas derived from the competency-based movement. Three major issues related to competency-based education are discussed herein: 1) what it is, 2) where it came from, and 3) where it is going.

CBE: What It Is

Competency-based education is based on the specification or definition of what constitutes competency in a given field. Usually a great deal of research is considered, when available, before competency levels are identified. The way in which the agreed-upon level of competency is communicated is through the use of specific, behavioral objectives for which criterion levels of performance have been established. Once the required behaviors have been specified, they are placed in a hierarchy leading from simple to complex, and then an instructional sequence is planned that will help the learner achieve the desired behaviors. When the learner is ready, a test or check of some sort is administered to determine if the required level of competency has been achieved.

In CBE, *time may vary, but achievement is held constant,* i.e., if the required criterion level of performance is one hundred

Joe Lars Klingstedt is Assistant Professor of Curriculum and Instruction at the University of Texas at El Paso.

percent accuracy, the learner does not "pass" with ninety percent accuracy. The criterion level is the same for all groups. This is based on the belief that competence should not be measured through the use of norm-referenced tests but rather through criterion-referenced approaches. As the nature or complexity of a field changes, the criterion levels have to be adjusted to meet the new situations. However, once they are established, they apply to everyone in the same way until they are changed.

In CBE, a major concern is to provide many alternate ways for the learner to accomplish the stated objectives. Psychology has yielded information which indicates that different individuals possess different learning styles. Since *the emphasis in CBE is on achievement of specified objectives and not the ranking of learners,* an effort is made to increase the probability of learner success by providing different instructional routes from which the learner may select the one most compatible with his or her unique learning style. In selecting a route to follow toward the accomplishment of an objective, the learner may be able to choose from a lecture, a list of selected readings, a videotape presentation, a slide-tape package, a programmed instruction manual, or numerous other options. Should the alternative selected by the learner prove unsuccessful, other experiences or options are usually available for the purpose of allowing a recycling process.

CBE: Where It Came From

The birth of competency-based education did not come as a surprise—indications of its impending arrival were present for some time. One of the early hints which can be singled out was the development of programmed instruction, designed to train people in a step-by-step manner so that they would reach a preconceived end. The labor pains really became acute at the time that performance-based education programs began to spring up across the country in response to the public cry for accountability. The demand for the specification of criterion levels of performance on the part of many funding agencies provided the final push that resulted in the delivery of competency-based education.

Ideas do not just materialize "out of the blue." They have a source—they are rooted in a pattern of thinking. The thought pattern that gave us CBE was Experimentalism. There are three fundamental ideas associated with Experimentalism: 1) the world is in constant change, 2) educational practice should be based on evidence provided by psychological data, and 3) man's psychological and sociological behavior is based on an economic and well-being motive.[1]

World in change. Experimentalists accept the idea that the world is in constant change. They use Darwin's *Origin of Species* as a source for this position. Darwin said that constant change is present in the environment and in order to survive an organism must adapt to the environment. Experimentalists look to the theory of evolution as a source for their thinking related to the environment, behavior and learning.

Educational practice based on psychological data. Another idea which the Experimentalists accept is the notion that educational practice should be in agreement with evidence provided by psychological data. The Experimental Psychologists came to the front with the acceptance of Experimentalism. Among others, Pavlov, Hull, Watson, Thorndike and Skinner are names frequently mentioned in Experimental Psychology. Taking the theory of evolution as their starting point, they, along with other Experimental Psychologists, provided psychological data which indicated that education is a step-by-step process moving from the simple to the complex. They said that to study man meant to study his behavior, and that man's behavior was a product of conditioning. Therefore, behavior modification through the use of operant conditioning became an accepted tool of educational psychologists. The stimulus-response-reward idea of operant conditioning is based on the assumption that everything is learned and nothing is innate.

Economic and well-being motive. The Experimentalists believe that man is a sociological as well as a biological animal, and as such is controlled, to some extent, by economic and well-being motives. These motives are the force behind one's sociological and psychological behavior. This economic and well-being motive concept became an especially strong force following the Depression of the thirties. With the Depression came a great threat to the American way of life, including the educational system. Experimentalists such as George Counts and Harold Rugg proposed that what was needed was a reconstruction of society along cultural lines. They said that there was a white collar top-heaviness in the country and, as a result, the public schools had drifted into the hands of the upper middle class. This was bad, they said, because traditional middle-class values were bad. What they called for was a bold new social experiment. Counts outlined the school's role in the task in his speech "Dare the Schools Build a New Social Order?" He felt the answer was "yes," and that the necessary financial support should be provided by the federal government. Dewey's scientific method was proposed as a tool to be used in solving social problems.

The Experimentalists, among whom John Dewey stands out as the central figure, believed in the pursuit of the good life, which was defined as a democracy of social cooperation. Because man is a social animal, one's economic and well-being status is always measured in relation to others. The Experimentalists believe that every man has the right to enough material things, as well as non-material entities, to insure his health and happiness.

Relationships between CBE and Experimentalism. What eventually evolved into competency-based education started out, as has been indicated, under the name of "performance-based" education. These developments in education were and are based on the Experimentalists' emphasis of studying man by scientifically studying his behavior. Performance-based education programs placed an emphasis on changing the learner's behavior or performance. From an emphasis on performances identified by "immediate suggestion," the movement became more focused and attempted to zero in on performances, arrived at through reason, which were designed to guarantee a given competency level. In the Experimentalist tradition, the method used to define competency was the same as Dewey's scientific method, e.g., in the area of teacher education the "felt difficulty" was that teachers were not being adequately prepared; the "immediate suggestion" varied according to the situation. Following the emotional reaction, reason was brought to bear and a hypothesis or "contemplative theory" was formulated. Following this, procedures were established for testing the hypothesis; and, finally, constant reexamination of the program was built in. Experimentalists would support this approach because of their faith in the scientific method and its role in research. The faith in research exhibited by people within the CBE movement indicates their confidence in the compatibility of psychological data and educational practice (a fundamental idea of Experimentalism).

Another Experimentalist justification for the CBE approach is related to the economic and well-being motive. When competence levels are spelled out in terms of criterion levels of performance, individuals pursuing the objectives know what the tasks are and they feel a sense of real accomplishment upon reaching the points at which they attain an endorsement of their ability to perform in a competent manner.

The use of behavioral objectives within the CBE programs relates to the Experimentalists' belief that learning is defined as a change in behavior. Because the Experimentalists believe that everything that is gained is learned, it is logical to specify which behaviors you wish to promote or change: CBE does exactly this. One of John Dewey's major points was that it is important to have a clearly defined purpose. He believed that purposes lead the way in the educational process.

When one looks at CBE's hierarchies of behaviors, the relationship to the Experimentalist belief that learning is a step-by-step process moving from simple to complex becomes obvious. Competency-based education, and its approach to learning, like programmed instruction, is justified, partially, on this basis.

The planning of the instructional sequence in CBE also reflects an Experimentalist View. Efforts are made to modify the behavior of the learner by providing learning experiences which are selected carefully and connected in a sequential fashion so as to guide the learner through each step in the proper order. As responses are rewarded, the learner is conditioned to respond in a given manner.

In CBE, pretests are usually administered to the learner to determine the existence of the desired behavior *or* to measure "readiness." Readiness, as used in this connotation, is related to psychological, sociological and biological factors, and it is a direct outgrowth of the thinking of Experimentalists such as Robert Havighurst. The readiness concept is also present in the idea that learners may take posttests whenever they want to. As opposed to the "teachable moment," this might be called the "testable moment."

One of John Dewey's major goals for education was to promote growth. In CBE this idea is apparent in the lack of emphasis on grades. The Experimentalists, especially Counts and Rugg, would like this lack of emphasis on grades, because grades and the competition for them represent "bad" middle-class values. Instead of an emphasis on ranking and grading, in CBE achievement is held constant and competency level performance is emphasized. Although achievement is held constant, the time taken to reach the criterion level may vary. Tests are not administered to all learners at a specific time for the purpose of ranking and grading them: they are administered when the learner is ready, for the purpose of determining one's competence. The criterion level does not vary; it is the same for everyone.

While criterion levels are absolute, they are not always *a priori*. They are generally based on experience, and their absoluteness is always related to a specific time and situation. Experimentalists recognize that the world is changing constantly, and they say the schools should be the ally of change. In CBE, criterion levels change as the situation demands. As research evidence is gathered, new hypotheses are formulated and tested and constantly reexamined.

In CBE, the idea of providing alternative learning routes for the student to follow in attempting to accomplish the stated objectives is related to psychological data which indicate that different people have different learning styles. The Experimentalists say, "Do not get in a rut: develop new alternatives." Competency-based education does this through the use of resource centers, technological aids and a variety of other experiences.

The use of technology in CBE is based on the Experimentalist notion that man is a tool user: technology is fundamental to teaching. Experimentalists would say, "Don't just learn from texts and teachers, learn from experiences." In addition, they would say that experiences should cause the learner to interact with what is learned. Learning alternatives in CBE are designed to do just this.

CBE: Where It Is Going

At the beginning of this chapter it was pointed out that while CBE is derived from educational justifications found in Experimentalism, it is not necessary for one to be an Experimentalist to utilize certain aspects of CBE. John Dewey said that ". . . any theory and set of practices is dogmatic which is not based upon critical examination of its own underlying principles."[2] Furthermore, anyone who is "looking ahead to a new movement in education . . . should think in terms of Education itself rather than in terms of some 'ism' about education, even such an 'ism' as 'progressivism' " [Experimentalism].[3] In light of this statement, made by the man considered by many to be the "father of Experimentalism," it would seem permissible and logical to assume that CBE can, and should, be viewed and utilized in different ways by educators adhering to thought patterns other than Experimentalism. While it is true that the major support for CBE will probably continue to come, for some time, from the Experimentalist camp, it is equally true that as the concept is explored and examined by growing numbers of people who will be affected by it, changes in emphasis and direction, as well as justifications, will no doubt surface.

For example, there is a feeling on the part of some that the Experimentalists' focus on behavior modification is too narrow and as a consequence they are missing a major value of CBE—its ability to emphasize the fundamental ideas of a given field. Those holding this belief might fall into a thought pattern identified by Strain as Process Structure philosophy. To illustrate how certain aspects of CBE might be justified and utilized from a point of view other than Experimentalism, a brief explanation of Process Structure philosophy is given below, followed by some comments relative to how the Process Structuralists might use CBE. The fundamental ideas associated with Process Structure philosophy are: 1) process, and 2) structure.[4]

Process. Whereas Experimentalism is tied to the theory of evolution, Process Structuralism is more closely associated with the new physics (Quantum Mechanics) and the theory of relativity. The concept of process is logically derived from Quantum Mechanics, which emphasizes the idea that the world is made up of energy—reality is energy. One of the main thinkers in Process Structuralism, Alfred North Whitehead, held that empty space does not exist and that matter is not static, i.e., everything is energy. Together, these two points indicate that existence itself is a process.

The idea of process is also related to Einstein's theory of relativity. The theory of relativity holds that the dimensions of size, time, space and motion are all relative. Truth itself is relative to how up-to-date your ideas are.

Structure. With all of the new ideas and data available, a problem of organization arose which led to the need for, and emphasis upon, structure. We human beings demand a structure, a theory by which we can live. The idea of man's living by theories is an aspect of the fundamental idea of structure, which in turn relates to cognitive psychology. Jerome Bruner, cognitive psychologist, said that teaching the fundamental structure of a subject is justified on the basis that: 1) it makes a subject more comprehensible, 2) it promotes memory, for unless detail is placed in a structured pattern it is soon forgotten, 3) it fosters "transfer of training," and 4) it narrows the gap between "advanced" and "elementary" knowledge.[5]

Competency-based education from a Process Structuralist's point of view. As it is defined and utilized by the Experimentalists, CBE would have only limited appeal for the Process Structuralists. However, with certain modifications and redefinitions the idea might be very attractive to them. Since the position taken herein is that CBE's focus is expanding to include ideas from a variety of camps, in addition to Experimentalism, the following is presented as an illustration of how another group, the Process

Structuralists, might look at CBE.

The concept of competence is one which would appeal to the Process Structuralists; however, they would look at competence differently than do the Experimentalists. Cognitive psychology, not experimental psychology, provides the answer to motivation and competence according to the Process Structuralists. Instead of ideas of motivation related to Darwin and the primary needs approach, the Process Structuralists would say that effective interaction with the environment, as perceived by the individual, is the key to motivation. This effective interaction is related to the concept of competence.[6] This competence or effectance motivation is related to manipulating the environment—unbalance, not balance, is the key. White says that we should not identify either pleasure or reinforcement with drive reduction, nor should we think of motivation as something that requires a source of energy external to the nervous system. He says that this makes the way clear for considering in their own right those aspects of animal and human behavior in which stimulation and contact with the environment are sought and welcomed: raised tension and mild excitement are cherished for their own sake. He states that effectance motivation should be the key to education. It must be conceived to involve satisfaction, a feeling of power in transaction in which behavior has an exploratory character and produces changes in the stimulus field. Possessing this character, the behavior leads the organism to find out how the environment can be changed and what consequences will result from these changes.[7]

For example, the student preparing for the teaching profession needs a variety of opportunities to interact in a variety of ways with learners. Beyond manual skills, many would say that the Experimentalists are on the wrong track in assuming that competencies can be identified in terms of specific behaviors. Consider teaching and the competencies associated with effective teaching. Few would argue that the appropriate criterion for measuring effective teaching is some type of pupil learning. However, learning is a very complex process, in which many variables interact, and in the absence of sufficient data indicating relationships between teacher behaviors and pupil learning, judgments concerning teacher competencies are often made on *a priori* grounds.

The Process Structuralists would say that the "answer" for which the Experimentalists are searching is not to be found. The world is changing and so are the answers. Furthermore, the answer to teaching competency varies with and is related to the individual teacher as well as the situation in which he or she is to function. Teachers in training do not need a set of pat answers. They do need a repertoire of behaviors, but not necessarily a common set for everyone. In addition, possessing any set of behaviors does not mean the prospective teachers will be competent automatically. Teaching competency is a function of style which is entirely unique with each individual.

Effectance motivation, not drive reduction, is a more reasonable approach to behaviors emphasized and equated with teaching competency. Within this frame of reference, the Process Structuralists would say that teaching intern teachers a *variety* of skills is good, providing they are viewed by the learners as valuable in providing opportunities to interact in many different ways with learners in such a way that the teachers and learners gain a feeling of efficacy. The way in which these competencies are identified for teacher education is in terms of the structure of teaching where effective interaction with the environment, not behavior modification, is the goal. Because a person's environment includes himself and his perceptions, as well as other people and objects, there can be no *one* formula for effective interaction. Just as one can learn the behaviors associated with good golfing and still not be able to put them together into an effective (winning) style, so too can teachers develop skills and not become effective in terms of a teaching style.

The Process Structuralists would say that CBE is a theory worthy of inspection, but it cannot prescribe an absolute answer. We can only get at partial truth and only relative to a particular situation and point in time. We always face uncertainty, but we struggle against it. Whitehead said, "Never swallow anything whole. We live perforce by half-truths and get along fairly well as long as we do not mistake them for whole-truths."[8] Hence, the Process Structuralists would not go for a uniform set of "competencies" for all teachers, as is proposed by many Experimentalists.

As has been indicated, the Process Structuralists would be in favor of CBE to the extent that it reveals the basic structure of the subject being taught. Strain says that "Structure involves the construction of categories from the world of events ... Man requires a system of theoretical structure in order to make use of the stimuli he receives from the environment ... Theories of this type are merely cognitive structures, not actual systems of nature. Thus they cannot exist indefinitely. New theories must replace old ones not because the old theories are proved wrong, but because they no longer explain adequately a growing body of data."[9] In talking about structure, Bruner says that "to learn structure, in short, is to learn how things are related."[10] Bruner believes that transfer is facilitated through the teaching and learning of structure rather than the mastery of facts.[11] The implication of this for teacher education would seem to be to emphasize the development of an effective style through an understanding and application of the fundamental ideas of teaching according to each individual's unique abilities. Don't attempt to provide answers to all of the questions before they are asked; rather, emphasize strategies, skills and techniques which the teacher can put together into his or her own unique style. The strategies, skills and techniques are not the end: competence or effective interaction with the environment is the goal, and each person may pursue a different path toward satisfaction of this objective. The set, fixed, inflexible road may be easier and it may promote a certain feeling of security, but learners will eventually find it non-stimulating. Whitehead said that " ... the broad primrose path leads to a nasty place. This evil path is represented by a book or a set of lectures which will practically enable the student to learn by heart all the questions likely to be asked at the next external examination."[12]

The Process Structuralists would agree that the teacher should have clearly defined objectives (a critical element in CBE). Whitehead said, "A certain ruthless definiteness is essential in education. I am sure that one secret of a successful teacher is that he has formulated quite clearly in his mind what the pupil has got to know in precise fashion. He will then cease from half-hearted attempts to worry his pupils with memorizing a lot of irrelevant stuff of inferior importance."[13] True as this may be, it should be emphasized that the Process Structuralists would not like a uniform set of specific, behavioral objectives to be used by everyone. This is supported by Whitehead when he states that "no absolutely rigid curriculum, not modified by its [the school's] own staff, should be permissible. Exactly the same principles apply, with the proper modifications, to universities and to technical colleges."[14]

Conclusion

In view of the evidence available, it should be obvious that CBE is a trend that is definitely catching on in educational circles. Laymen as well as teachers are "tuning in" to this kind of thinking. Several states are changing teacher certification requirements in the direction of clearly specified competencies which must be mastered before the certificate will be issued. As has been pointed out, although CBE has its roots in Experimentalism, educators embracing other positions can, and perhaps should, exert an influence on CBE's ultimate direction. By selecting and emphasizing those aspects of CBE which are most closely related to their own thought patterns, educators can influence the ultimate result of an emphasis on CBE. In this way CBE's long-range effects may be far more significant than if utilized and examined only within the Experimentalist frame of reference.

Notes

1. Strain, John Paul. *Modern Philosophies of Education.* New York: Random House, 1971, 65-68. The explanation of Experimentalism presented herein is derived from this source as well as personal conversations and learning interactions with the author (John Paul Strain).
2. Dewey, John. *Experience and Education.* New York: The Macmillan Company, 1938, 22.   ‒

3. *Ibid.*, 6.
4. Strain. *Op. cit.*, 174-178. The explanation of Process Structure philosophy presented herein is derived from this source as well as personal conversations and learning interactions with the author (John Paul Strain).
5. Bruner, Jerome. *The Process of Education.* New York: Random House, 1960, 23-26.
6. White, Robert. Motivation Reconsidered—The Concept of Competence. *Psychological Review, 16* (1959), 267-333.
7. *Ibid.*
8. Price, Lucien. *Dialogues of Alfred North Whitehead.* New York: New American Library of World Literature, 1964, 243.
9. Strain. *Op. cit.*, 175-176.
10. Bruner. *Op. cit.*, 7.
11. *Ibid.*
12. Whitehead, Alfred North. *The Aims of Education.* New York: The Free Press, 1929, 4-5.
13. *Ibid.*, 36.
14. *Ibid.*, 14.

3

Psychological Implications of Competency-Based Education

Jon I. Young and
Adrian P. Van Mondfrans

The accepted procedures of competency-based and conventional education systems differ considerably. Conventional education relies heavily on the teacher or text to dispense knowledge geared toward the average students, with few provisions made for the slower or faster students. In competency-based education the responsibility is often placed on the student to initiate the learning by using the teacher as a resource person. In addition, a competency-based education system is not dependent on the concept of class advancement; any student may select goals more or less sophisticated than those of his peer social group.

Table 1 itemizes some of the basic differences between these two educational systems. These differences are evident in the amount of choice allowed students with respect to goals and instructional and evaluation procedures, the amount of information given students concerning the instructional goals, and the sensitivity of the system to individual differences. Some of the questions related to these differences concern the changes in student affect from an increased autonomy and added sensitivity to how these changes affect performance. These questions are examined under specific psychological topics in light of existing theory and data.

Interest

Interests have been defined as "a readiness to be concerned

Jon I. Young is at the University of Maine at Orono. **Adrian P. Van Mondfrans** is at Brigham Young University, Provo, Utah.

Table 1

A Comparison of Competency-Based and Conventional Systems of Instruction

	COMPETENCY-BASED	CONVENTIONAL
1. Who sets the goals and objectives of instruction?	Both the teacher and student are usually involved. When the teacher sets the goals and objectives the student is told what they are and often is allowed some choice of objective or goal.	The teacher usually sets the goals and objectives. Often they are not clearly defined. Students are usually not told what they are. Students usually do not have a choice.
2. Who decides on the means and procedures of instruction?	Students often have a choice of alternative routes, experiences and materials to use in pursuing a given goal or objective. The student controls the amount of time spent on the goal or objective.	The teacher usually controls the situation and presents all students with the same materials and experiences for the same amount of time.
3. What is learned?	Students usually learn how to do something.	Students may learn about something.
4. Who decides on the evaluation procedures?	The teacher ensures that the evaluation procedures are consistent with the objectives. Often the student has a choice of ways to demonstrate that he can perform as expected.	The teacher usually gives a test of his or her own design. Students often don't know what is expected of them. Testing procedures tend to be paper-and-pencil tests.
5. When does evaluation take place?	When the student indicates he is ready.	When the teacher is through teaching a unit of instruction.
6. When does the student move on to the next set of learning goals and objectives?	When the student has mastered the last set of objectives and goals. The student continues working on a set of goals or objectives until mastery is achieved.	When the last unit has been taught and the evaluation of students is completed. Students may have "failed" or "passed" the last unit at various levels of proficiency. Nevertheless, all students move on to new content.

with or moved (motivated) by an object or class of objects" (Webster's Seventh New Collegiate Dictionary, 1969). This readiness to be involved has long been recognized as a valuable asset in increasing learning. Interests may first be manifested as curiosity and then developed into personal commitments. White (1959) recognized curiosity as a cause of exploratory behaviors and an important intrinsic motivator. Curiosity is sustained when continued interest evolves into personal commitment. Heslin and Blake (1969) have shown that performance improves as a student becomes personally committed to the task and personal commitment is much more evident when students are allowed to select their own goals.

Another aspect of interest is that it can inspire students with low educational backgrounds to perform at desired levels as quickly as students with high educational backgrounds (Marshall, 1969).

Interest cannot be guaranteed by any educational system but its likelihood can be affected. Under conventional educational systems the likelihood of interests developing is restricted. The emphasis is often on vaguely defined and largely uninteresting material (Marx and Tombough, 1967). All the students learn it the same way, at the same time, making little allowance for individual tastes or abilities. The students are restricted in their choices, which limits their commitment to the task. It is difficult for them to pursue topics they become curious about.

In competency-based systems the student is an equal partner with the teacher. Although he may be expected to learn predetermined material, he is encouraged to select unique goals which consider his prerequisite knowledge. He is involved in the actual decision-making process about his education. Thus, a personal commitment is made for each goal by the student. This commitment may come in the form of an original goal design or in deciding between two "teacher sponsored" goals. Either way, it is the student's decision.

The spirit of competition, another form of interest, can be a potent motivator. Although competition is frequently employed under conventional systems, it is between students, while in competency-based education it is within the student. Students appear to prefer to compete with themselves. However, the situation must be set up so the student knows what his past performance is and can monitor current progress on a daily basis. He must set up goals for competition within himself, and then achievement of them will motivate him to do more.

Motivation

Motivation is obviously the key to solving many educational ills. Motivation is described as some inner will to act or accomplish something.

Conventional education recognizes the importance of motivation, and teachers employ such techniques as rewards, recognitions and grades for excellence to stimulate it. Yet, it has long been recognized that it is the internal motivators that are most important. The conventional system forces each student to follow a class pattern. Students only have one opportunity to demonstrate their knowledge of a particular area, and often the external rewards become so important that cheating is used to achieve the goals.

Competency-based systems have the same need for motivated students. The material is not forced on students, and teachers are not required to use external motivators. Competency-based systems offer several advantages. The possibilities for creativity engendered by the system motivate students.

Within the framework of the teacher's expectations, students may select their own routes to developing these performances and use their own strategies to learn skills. The environment is non-threatening, since the student is not concerned with whether he will pass or fail; he can take all the time he needs and make as many attempts as necessary to achieve the goal. The system also allows for more intra-personal competition.

Frustration

Frustration is frequently defined as a condition which results when a subject is blocked from reaching a goal (Marx and Tombough, 1967). The internal force that propels a student toward a goal is called drive, and a detrimental effect on learning occurs when the drive is thwarted (Goldman, Keck and O'Leary, 1969; Hinton, 1968). Classical learning theorists, such as Hull, have indicated that a goal-directed drive is a critical element in learning (Hull, 1943). Atkinson and Feather (1966), have suggested that frustration interferes with goal-oriented drives by dissipating their directiveness and making them too general to be effective. Since a personal commitment toward a goal produces a strong goal-directed drive, it would follow that blocking this drive would cause acute frustration. This frustration might even intensify if the goal was blocked and no alternative approaches were available.

Under conventional systems, frustration is created when teacher goals conflict with student goals. This is often the case because teacher goals are deemed more important. The problem is further complicated because there normally exists one method of achieving the goal: Attend class and take the test. However, since the student is forced to accept the teacher's goals, his frustration is minimal, because he may never be totally committed. Competency-based education purports to allow the student the freedom to select his own goals; therefore, frustration would be intensified if the student didn't have alternate means of achieving the goal in case of failure or blocking. Alternate procedures mean that if the student fails in an initial attempt, he need not return to the same instructional material but may elect to pursue some other learning alternative.

The ambiguity and irrelevancy that often surround conventional programs are often factors affecting frustration. The student is often not sure what he is expected to be able to do, and if he does know, he isn't sure whether it is worth his effort to wade through all the material his teacher believes to be essential.

Another inherent characteristic of the conventional system is the high level of frustration. Students are given one chance to achieve on a test. Failure means disgrace and no chance of modifying the outcome. In competency-based environments there is no failure. If a student doesn't achieve a goal the first time, he tries again until he succeeds. The alternative routes to the goal make further unacceptable performances the student's responsibility and not the teacher's. Frustration can be further reduced under competency-based instruction if tolerances are built up (Atkinson and Feather, 1966) by allowing the student to slowly increase task difficulty (McCandless, 1967). The task to be performed need not change to vary the difficulty, but the criterion level of achievement may be slowly altered so the student won't feel overwhelmed with the task. Since the goal of this system is to measure student achievement in terms of competencies, the student may repeat the task as often as necessary. With each attempt, the criterion level can be slightly increased until the desired level of mastery is demonstrated. Another advantage of this approach is the student's positive reinforcement experience from success on every attempt, which minimizes failures.

One attempt to alleviate the frustration of failure by the conventional system is to eliminate holding students back due to low grades. The student thus remains with his peer group whether or not he meets the academic standards. McCandless (1967) says this action prevents social frustration but may create the academic frustration of being above or below the scope of the instruction.

Competency-based systems attempt to eliminate both problems by allowing students of the same age group to be actively pursuing goals above or below their peer level. Only the teacher and the students involved need be aware of level of achievement.

Anxiety

Anxiety is an emotional predisposition. Too much anxiety normally reduces a student's effectiveness, while moderate anxiety increases his effectiveness. Many studies have pointed out the advantages of understanding anxiety (Levy, Gooch and Dellmer-Pringle, 1969; Cottle, 1969; O'Neil, Spielberger and Hansen, 1969; Chabassol and Thomas, 1967, 1968; Harleston, 1962).

The conclusions of two other studies suggest the implications of anxiety on educational systems. Lott and Lott (1968) indicated that manifest anxiety doesn't affect performance, and Harleston (1962) indicated that situational anxiety (test anxiety) does. It is obvious that if situational anxiety can be controlled, performance will improve. The important point here is that the situational anxiety which is crucial to learning is tied to a specific situation. The teacher doesn't need to practice therapeutic techniques to reduce manifest anxiety, but he can alter the characteristics of a specific situation.

The Yerkes-Dodson Law (Yerkes and Dodson, 1908) states that the more complex a task becomes, the lower the student's drive level. The more complex a task, the more anxiety a student feels; and the more anxiety increases, the more random the student's behavior becomes. The fact that complex tasks reduce effective performance may also be attributed to stress, which has an indirect effect on anxiety (Marx and Tombough, 1967). In either case, poor performance on complex tasks stems from an uncertainty of the situation, which promotes feelings of inadequacy, which in turn increases anxiety.

With conventional educational systems it is the nature of the test-taking environment that increases situational anxiety through the uncertainty of the situation. All the students must take the test at the same time and without any concrete information on what is expected. Anxiety is further increased because there is generally only one chance to succeed in the conventional testing system.

Competency-based education, however, besides informing the student of precisely what is expected, may even allow him to examine the task prior to showing his competency. There are several advantages to this type of procedure. First, the student receives all available clues (McCandless, 1967). Studies on prompting (Merrill and Tennyson, 1971) and review (Young, 1972) with concept acquisition tasks indicate that both these procedures significantly reduce a student's inaccurate responses. According to McCandless, this result may be attributable to the student's reduced anxiety.

Second, the more a student has control over the test-taking procedures, the better he performs (Neale and Katahn, 1968). Part of having control is being certain of what the situation involves.

Self-Concept

Although self-concept is often difficult to define, it is rather widely accepted that the construct is learned. A person develops a positive self-concept in proportion to the positive reinforcement he receives for his performances. There is some evidence that self-concept has some commonalities with drive (McCandless, 1967) in that certain activities are selected based on certain self-concept characteristics. This conceptual framework is supported by Walsh (1956) when she concluded that children with low self-concepts perceive themselves as being restricted and not free to pursue their own interests.

Academically, Coopersmith (1959) found a significant correlation between positive self-concept and achievement, and that students with a high self-concept were less anxious. Since it has been pointed out earlier that anxiety can be reduced and student autonomy increased under a competency-based educational system, it follows that this system would be most conducive to the formulation of a positive self-concept.

Festinger (1957) supports this conclusion in that he reports self-concept will become more positive if the behavior is positive, is accompanied by a high degree of freedom of choice or occurs under low pressure. Furthermore, the reduction of negative or failing experiences by the student increases positive self-concepts. All of these variables form an integral part of competency-based education.

Conclusion

The purpose of education—to train students to be self-motivated learners—cannot be fully realized as long as the instructional goals are teacher goals. Real-life situations will not have a teacher available to tell students what to do. These situations will involve individual responsibility for personally selected goals.

Although competency-based education involves high risks because of reduced teacher direction and increased student control, the rewards are great. This system can reduce negative psychological effects and increase learning.

References

Atkinson, John W. and Norman T. Feather. *Achievement Motivation.* New York: John Wiley and Sons, 1966.

Carlson, J.S. and F.L. Ryan. Levels of Cognitive Functioning as Related to Anxiety. *Journal of Experimental Education,* 37 (1969), 17-20.

Chabassol, David J. and David C. Thomas. Anxiety, Aptitude, Achievement and Performance in Female Teachers. *Alberta Journal of Educational Research,* 13:4 (1967), 291-294.

Chabassol, David J. and David C. Thomas. Anxiety, Aptitude, Achievement and Performance in Male Elementary Teachers. *Alberta Journal of Educational Research,* 14:4 (1968), 233-237.

Coopersmith, S. A Method for Determining Types of Self-Esteem. *Journal of Educational Psychology,* 59 (1959), 87-94.

Cottle, Thomas J. Temporal Correlates of the Achievement Value and Manifest Anxiety. *Journal of Consulting Clinical Psychology,* 33:5 (1969), 541-550.

Festinger, L. *Theory of Cognitive Dissonance.* Evanston, Illinois: Row, Peterson, 1957.

Frandsen, Arden and Maurice Sorenson. Interests as Motives in Academic Achievement. *Journal of School Psychology,* 7:1 (1968-1969), 52-56.

Goldman, Morton, Jonathan W. Keck and Charles J. O'Leary. Hostility Reduction and Performance. *Psychological Reports,* 25-2 (1969), 503-512.

Harleston, Bernard W. Test Anxiety and Performance in Problem-Solving Situations. *Journal of Personality,* 30 (1962), 557-573.

Heslin, Richard and Brian Blake. Performance as a Function of Payment, Commitment and Task Interest. *Psychonomic Science,* 15:6 (1969), 323-324.

Hinton, Bernard L. Environmental Frustration and Creative Problem-Solving. *Journal of Applied Psychology,* 52:3 (1968) 211-217.

Hull, C.L. *Principles of Behavior.* New York: Appleton-Century-Crofts, 1943.

Levy, Philip, Stan Gooch and M.J. Dellmer-Pringle. A Longitudinal Study of the Relationship Between Anxiety and Streaming in a Progressive and a Traditional Junior School. *British Journal of Educational Psychology,* 39:2 (1969), 166-173.

Lott, Bernice E. and Albert J. Lott. The Relation of Manifest Anxiety in Children to Learning Task Performance and Other Variables. *Child Development,* 39:1 (1968), 207-220.

Marshall, Hermine H. Learning as a Function of Task Interest, Reinforcement and Social Class Variables, *Journal of Educational Psychology,* 60:2 (1969), 133-137.

Marx, Melvin H. and Tom N. Tombough. *Motivation.* San Francisco: Chandler, 1967.

McCandless, Boyd R. *Children's Behavior and Development.* New York: Holt, Rinehart and Winston, 1967.

Merrill, M.D. and R.D. Tennyson. Attribute Prompting Variables in Learning Classroom Concepts. *Final Report of USOE Small Contract 0-11-014,* September 1971.

Neale, John M. and Martin Katahn. Anxiety, Choice and Stimulus Uncertainty. *Journal of Personality,* 36:2 (1968), 235-245.

O'Neil, Harold F., Jr., Charles D. Spielberger and Duncan F. Hansen. Effects of State Anxiety and Task Difficulty on Computer Assisted Learning. *Journal of Educational Psychology,* 60:5 (1969), 343-350.

Walsh, Ann M. *Self-Concepts of Bright Boys with Learning Difficulties.* New York: Bureau of Publications, Teachers College, Columbia University, 1956.

White, R.W. Motivation Reconsidered: The Concept of Competence. *Psychological Review,* 66 (1959), 297.

Yerkes, R.M. and J.D. Dodson. The Relation of Strength of Stimulus to Rapidity of Habit Formation. *Journal of Comparative and Neurological Psychology,* 18 (1908), 459-482.

Young, Jon I. The Effects of Review Techniques and Instance Presentation on Concept Learning Tasks. Paper presented at American Educational Research Association. Annual Meeting, Chicago, April 1972.

4

Competency-Based Learning:
An Analysis of Polyadic Interaction

Ronald V. Kidd
and Luiz F.S. Natalicio

This chapter is an attempt to interpret competency-based learning from a psychological point of view. What is "psychological" has often been misinterpreted; therefore, what is to be understood as psychological in this chapter is the study or analysis of behavioral interaction. What is psychological is something not about the specific individuals who behave but about the behavioral interactions of individuals. An individual's behavior does not provide grounds upon which to make inferences about the individual; what the individual does, his behavior, is analyzable in its own right. All that is meant by "polyadic" is that the behavioral interaction of more than two individuals is the subject of study. An obvious example of polyadic interaction is the play of a football team.

Any analysis of behavioral interaction concerns the transient outcomes of specific interactions as well as the changes which occur in the quality of these interactions over a period of time. For example, a young football team may play better as a team later in the season; they are said to have "gelled." However, any particular play any time during the season may be analyzed in and of itself. Analogously, with respect to competency-based learning, one is necessarily concerned with the qualitative changes in polyadic behavioral interactions over a rather extended period of time. One is interested in how well the interaction has approxi-

Ronald V. Kidd is Assistant Professor of Educational Psychology at the University of Texas at El Paso. **Luiz F.S. Natalicio** is Associate Professor of Education at the University of Texas at El Paso.

mated the performance standards overlaid upon it. "Competent," then, is a descriptive label one applies to an interaction when it has approximated the standard or the behavioral criterion. One might say the interaction has "gelled." Competency-based learning is simply a summary label applied to the ongoing sequence of particular interactions which have been systematically designed to approach and finally to approximate the particular performance standards. However, one must not be misled; continuing analyses of the particular transient interactions are part of the systematic design. In short, then, any ongoing sequence of polyadic, behavioral interactions can be analyzed from a systems (i.e., psychological) point of view. A simple systems diagram is shown in Figure 1.

Figure 1

Simple Systems Diagram

Learning is the process component of the system. Every time one analyzes the process, he assumes that the process has stopped. He compares the current performance state of the process with the standard performance which by design is to have occurred at this particular point in time in the development ("maturation") of the interaction. All the familiar problems of assessment or measurement arise here, and these problems are considered in numerous other chapters (e.g., Burns, this book). One of the concerns of a psychological study is how the comparisons or assessments one makes are made part of the process. This feature of a systems analysis is called corrective (or degenerative) feedback. The one who participates in the behavioral interaction in making the comparisons must be considered to function as the feedback loop in the system, as seen in Figure 2.

Figure 2

Diagram of Feedback Subprocess

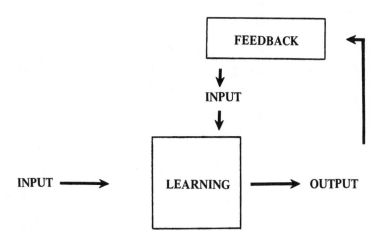

Feedback to the football team comes not only after each play but also at halftime and during the following practices through coaching and other corrective interventions.

This feedback must become a part of the process. It must be input into the process. When the process is stopped in order to assess its current state, what is assessed must be considered the output of the system at that time. The difficulty of giving feedback in polyadic behavioral interactions is due to the complexity of such interactions. Input to behavioral systems is not only the curricular materials and other situational variables in the usual classroom, for instance, but also the behavior of many other individuals, including the students. Feedback subsequent to static comparisons is simply one of these many parts of the total input. Hence, considering polyadic interaction as a complex system made up of many subsystems with subprocesses, feedback serves its corrective function effectively when it is given with respect to as many of the subprocesses as possible. For example, the defensive backfield coach gives feedback only with respect to the interaction of the defensive backfield.

However, each subsystem is interacting with other sub-systems. The integrity of the system as a functioning unit depends on subsystem interaction. Compensatory feedback to other subsystems which are affected by the inefficient functioning of one subsystem is usually ineffective. Compensatory feedback anticipates the disintegration of the whole system. For example, when the backfield coach does a poor job of providing corrective feedback, shoring up the defensive line does little in the way of compensating for the inefficiency of the backfield system. At the end of an unsuccessful season, moreover, not only the backfield coach, but the head coach as well may no longer be part of the system.

The purpose of this systems approach is to emphasize that "competency" is only a state or static descriptive label, whereas learning involves a process or dynamic description. A systems approach is a psychological approach when it describes the process of learning. And learning, except where it is tutorial (or dyadic), is a process in which many individuals interact; i.e., it is a sequence of changes in the quality of polyadic interaction. Competencies are not features of, products of, or anything that can be found in interaction. Competencies are labels given to results of a comparison of a particular performance *state* of a process with a static performance standard or behavioral criterion. Competencies are inferences, then, and each competency is only inferentially related to the learning process from which the static comparison is derived. Hence, competencies are not measures of learning. They are labels given to product comparison. Comparisons of processes are not attempted.

These limitations are crucial when one undertakes the design of a system in which the process is to lead to some prespecified state of the system. Competencies, to repeat, are labels given to the comparison of the measurable output of this process of synthesis with some predetermined performance standard. When one considers competencies to be that which is synthesized, he is making excessive claims for a process, only the static description of which has anything to do with the notion of competency. The interpretation of competency-based learning that this chapter attempts is one which retains the integrity of learning, the process itself, and relegates the notion of competency to a function as part of the corrective feedback loop to each of the many systems' subprocesses.

In short, competency-based learning seems preoccupied with synthesis, how to manufacture a standard product. In looking at a system as a process of synthesis, for example, one might look at the owner of a football team as a buyer of raw material that the coach refines, molds and assembles into a precision unit. The process, i.e., the play of the team, has become secondary to the product to be synthesized, i.e., the state of the team. When one considers competency-based learning to be a form of polyadic interaction, then he contents himself with analysis and with the process itself, in which many different individuals and many different things participate in a variety of ways. Besides systems analysis, behavioral analysis or operant analysis details how one might monitor interventions (feedback) into ongoing processes.

Systems tend toward rigidity and ritualism. That is, after a while the processes that go on in the system begin to look the same over and over again. The output from these rigid systems is stereotypic. The system puts its stamp on the input, and that stamp is carried through the process to become part of the output. For example, when a football team matures, it plays with a certain style (stereotypically), and the players on the team are thereby stamped as players of that style. Whether or not mature systems are preferable to more flexible systems in which the performance standard changes with respect to the process itself is part of the evaluative subprocesses in the system. No analysis can construct an evaluation of a system or its processes. An analysis can only describe the process as it occurs.

In summary, competency-based learning is a process, just as any other form of behavioral interaction is a process. The notion of basing learning on competency is facilitative to learning when comparisons of the performance standards to momentary output from the process function as part of corrective feedback to the system. Competencies are analyzed as the process by which the output from comparisons comes to be transformed into corrective feedback. Analysis is the method of choice in the study of these systems as opposed to a method which considers the synthesized product. From a psychological point of view, then, competency-based learning is analyzed as the process of behavioral interaction among a number of individuals over an undefined period of time. Monitoring the direction the process is taking and the changes that are occurring in the interactions may include a subprocess in which the notion of competency is considered. However, the notion of competency serves the process; the process is not subservient to the notion of competency.

5

Empathy Competence:
A Search for New Direction
in Canadian Teacher Education

P.G. Halamandaris
and A. John Loughton

Teacher Education in Canada is a function of conservative faculties of education in which significant program change rarely occurs. What does occur is a great deal of rhetoric about the direction of potential change. Such talk is often complemented by the manipulation of existing formats. For example, student teaching may be moved from third year to first year, or from eight weeks to fourteen weeks. But the student anxiety caused by this relatively short period of field experience and the rigorous evaluation procedure which usually accompanies it, remains. Courses become electives instead of requirements—but other "courses" are created in their place. The assumption remains that courses as we know them are relevant to teacher education programs. Certification requirements are often changed simply by increasing the minimum number of courses done at a University— reflecting the erroneous principle that somehow academic achievement as it is presently conceived and measured is a valid *indicator-predictor* of future teacher competence. Further, if changes such as pass-fail grading or modular programs are implemented, a formula is usually included which allows these experiences to be translated back into courses and grades on transcripts so that such activities can be "properly" evaluated. Thus teacher education in Canada appears anachronistically

P.G. Halamandaris is Associate Professor and Director of Educational Research, Faculty of Education, Brandon University. **A. John Loughton** is Assistant Professor, Faculty of Education, Brandon University.

embedded in the traditional university classroom.

Competency-based education is an emerging phenomenon in Canadian teacher education. Unfortunately, it is often ushered into faculties of education under the assumption that the objectives of teacher education are best achieved solely by the acquisition of learning strategies. A lack of reasonable balance between *skill-competence* and *empathy-competence* may result in the kind of indictment produced by Nash (1970, p. 240) in his assessment of competency-based programs:

> In an overzealousness born out of frustration and defensiveness we are adopting a model which promises to bestow a magical kind of scientific-technological warrant on our professional endeavors. What is happening, however, is that we are fetishizing and trivializing an entire teacher education program.

A great deal of time, energy and effort is spent in the area of cognitive and psychomotor skill acquisition by potential teachers. Obviously, the potential teacher must possess such *skill-competence*. A teacher must have expertise in a subject matter area. However, it is absolutely essential that the student teacher not consider the transmission of cognitive skills as his sole responsibility.

Personality characteristics of student teachers, such as empathy, openness, maturity and the potential ability to relate to children, peers and/or parents, have been neglected in traditional teacher education programs. The ideal teacher must be first and foremost the possessor of *empathy-competence. Empathy-competence* may be defined as the ability of a teacher to genuinely consider, as a first priority, the rights, feelings and achievements of the individual student, in all teaching activities. The implication for teacher education programs seems clear. There must be included in the design of such programs ways of initiating, supporting and evaluating the potential *empathy-competence* of student teachers.

A balance between *empathy-competence* and *skill-competence* must exist in teacher education. Presently, faculties of education in Canada rarely ascertain whether or not student teachers even *like* children, let alone have an empathy potential. A rather horrifying possibility, albeit hyperbole, is the proposition that a reasonably bright psychopath could be certified with ease in the Province of Manitoba or any other Canadian province. By default, certification requirements neglect to evaluate how the student teacher relates to others. If he is able to pass prescribed courses and survive the relatively short term of superficial anxiety that we call "student teaching," he will be certified.

Obviously, there are some difficulties in the identification and measurement of personality traits as they apply to teacher education. However, evidence (Getzels and Jackson, 1963; Combs, 1962) supports the need for exploration in such areas as "attitudinal correlates of ability." The most plausible formula for an evaluation of such characteristics at the present time seems to be a lengthy period of internship, with the supervising personnel responsible for a cooperative recommendation *vis-a-vis empathy-competence* at the completion of this internship. The evaluation of *empathy-competence* of the student teacher is done most effectively by having the student work in a teaching and learning center in close contact with his students, supervisors and peers for this extended period. At the end of this time the supervising staff should be able to make recommendations about his capacity for empathy. Another source of evidence used in this evaluation process is a student self-evaluation of his competence. The student's faculty tutor, an individual who has been an *advisor-confidant* of the student throughout his program, would then be charged with the responsibility for the combined evaluation.

To meet the teacher education needs in Canada in the 1970s, education must include a community dimension, i.e., not only within the institution of the school, but also in the larger social milieu. The assumption here is that an individual's teaching competence, both real and potential, can be best supported if he participates in the planning, implementing and evaluating of classroom and community experience.

Because of the conservative nature of Canadian teacher education, it appears that it may be easier to initiate change through the establishment of the existing format, than to attempt to reform the existing structure. One such attempt to implement change in Manitoba is the IMPACTE (Indian and Metis Project for Careers through Teacher Education) program at Brandon University. IMPACTE is a teacher education program designed to meet the Provincial (Manitoba) certification requirements. An IMPACTE student could meet such requirements in approximately two-and-one-half to three years and in some instances earlier. All the students participating in this program are Canadians of either Indian or Metis descent.

Certainly a prime principle underlying the establishment of a program for persons of native ancestry is to educate people who have a large amount of *empathy-competence* potential. The selection and education of these Canadians as teachers is dependent in no small part on the conviction that an Indian or Metis child should have a school experience that will provide him with the same life chances as majority Canadians. This is not to say that the goal of these equal life chances is assimilation, but rather that the goal is to provide the native child with the ability to make choices as to life style and occupation with the same degree of self-determination as other Canadians. Crucial to the acquisition of this status is the existence of *significant others* who will act as models for the child during the school experience.

Obviously, the racial identity of student teachers does not insure that they will be able to provide significant models for Indian and Metis children. However, a self-selection of these individuals as potential teachers, coupled with recommendations of members of their community, should be a reasonable indication of the individual's normative acquaintance with the values, beliefs, mores and language of the native community.

The skill competency of these potential teachers must not be overlooked. The open admission policy of the IMPACTE Project results in a student body with widely varied academic backgrounds. Recognition of this has generated a number of supportive services and administrative arrangements that facilitate the learning experience for students. In order to provide the students with the skills that will allow them to perform at a satisfactory level in the classroom, tutorial services are a necessary component of the program. Some IMPACTE courses are designed to meet the individual needs of the student through a modular format. In these modules the time factor is variable, while the achievement or performance level is held constant. Therefore, an emphasis of IMPACTE is on the successful acquisition of skill competence, and students within the project are able to take more time if necessary to perform at this satisfactory level. The problems of measuring performance over a specified period of time are then avoided by allowing the student to complete course requirements whenever he meets the performance standards.

The emphasis on practicum is based partly upon the principle that the connection between practical experience and academic work provides the student with the chance to see himself more clearly as a teacher. He becomes more and more involved with his tasks, while at the same time he is able to perceive himself as a contributor to the community. Further, this teacher education program is to produce professionals who can reflect the needs of the local community. Therefore, IMPACTE incorporates a work-study program which combines ten to fifteen hours a week of actual classroom experience for the trainee as an instructional assistant. The student participates in community development course work at the university which requires that he, during the summer, participate actively within his own community in such areas as community recreation, adult literacy, pre-school education (Head Start-type project) or politics.

In conclusion, relevance of teacher education programs in Canada in the 1970s will depend to a significant degree upon the acquisition by student teachers of both *empathy-competence* and *skill-competence*. One way of achieving such competence is through a program of community involvement. Positive differences in these two areas may be provided by IMPACTE. If so, IMPACTE may provide positive data that should help overcome the vagary of defining personality characteristics and their use in teacher education, and further support the prognosis that *empathy-competence* is a priority consideration for effective teacher education in Canada in the future.

References

Combs, A.W. The Self in Chaos. A Review of Wylie, R.C., The Self Concept. A Critical Survey of Pertinent Research Literature. *Contemporary Psychology.* 7 (1962), 53-54.

Dreeben, Robert. *On What Is Learned in Schools.* Don Mills, Ontario: Addison-Wesley Publishing Company, 1968.

Fine, Sidney A. *Guidelines for the Employment of the Culturally Disadvantaged.* W.E. Upjohn Center for Employment Research, Kalamazoo, Michigan, June 1969.

Getzels, J.W. and P.W. Jackson. The Teacher's Personality and Characteristics. In N.L. Gage (Ed.) *Handbook of Research on Teaching.* Chicago: Rand McNally, 1963, 506-582.

Gold, Milton J. Opening the Doors to Teacher Education. *Peabody Journal of Education,* October 1971, 29-34.

Kinch, John W. A Formalized Theory of Self-Concept. *American Journal of Sociology,* January 1963, 481-486.

Knowell, Dorothy M. *Toward Educational Opportunity for All.* Albany: State University of New York, 1966.

Nash, Robert J. Commitment to Competency: The New Fetishism in Teacher Education. *Phi Delta Kappan,* December 1970, 240-243.

Purkey, William W. *Self-Concept and School Achievement.* Englewood Cliffs, New Jersey: Prentice-Hall, 1970.

Willingham, Warren W. Educational Opportunity and the Organization of Higher Education. *Barriers to Higher Education.* New York: College Entrance Examinations Board, 1971.

6

Behavioral Objectives for
Competency-Based Education

Richard W. Burns

Introduction

The most striking feature of competency-based education obviously is competency, which is synonomous with the concept of
ability. At the end of instruction, in competency education, the
learner is to have acquired the ability or skill to *do*—do
something—since doing is the essence of learning.

Learning can be defined as: Change in Behavior and/or Desire
to Behave. The competency movement is loaded with adjectives
and nouns signifying the important role of or emphasis on
behavior; "shaping behavior," "behavior modification," "terminal
behaviors," "behavioral objectives," "performance and behavior
criteria" are a few of the descriptive terms. It is the specification
of the behaviors to be acquired that gives leverage to the
competency-based movement. It is this extra power—this exact
specification of the behaviors to be acquired by the learner—that is
making the competency-based education movement more than
just another fad in the field of education.

The specified behaviors are most commonly called "objectives." Objectives are descriptions, in behavioral terms, of what the
learner is to be able to do at the end of any instructional period.
For this reason they are frequently referred to as *terminal
behavioral objectives* (TBOs). This chapter deals briefly with what
objectives are, reactions to selected criticisms concerning objec-

Richard W. Burns is Professor of Education at the University of Texas at El
Paso.

tives and their use, how objectives are related to accountability, uses of objectives, standards of performance, objectives and evaluation, and limitations relating to objectives.

Not all educators have embraced the competency movement, with its objectified structure. A variety of objections have been put forward against the use of objectives including the fact that they are too specific, dehumanizing, they over-emphasize trivia, they are too time-consuming to construct and just plain not descriptive of what education is really all about. Experience with both objectives and their critics tends to make one believe that some misunderstanding of what objectives are, what they can do and what they can be like when properly expressed is the cause of the criticism *rather than any inherent deficiency in or with objectives per se.*

What Are TBOs Like?

Before moving to important considerations involving the use of objectives—their role and application in competency education—it is necessary to pin down briefly what a TBO is as referred to in this chapter.* *A terminal behavioral objective* is a straightforward, written statement expressed from the learner's point of view describing the exact behavior (and the conditions under which the behavior will operate) the learner is to exhibit at the end of a period of instruction. A TBO is, in summary, specific, expressed from the learner's point of view and behaviorally descriptive. Here is an example:

TBO—High School—General Biology
Learners are to develop an understanding of the relationship of living things to their environment and to each other so that they can:
a.   Express in their own words the meaning of these terms:
     1. ecology, 2. symbiosis, 3. parasiticism, 4. food chain,

---

*For a comprehensive treatment of objectives see Burns, Richard W. *New Approaches to Behavioral Objectives.* Dubuque, Iowa: Wm. C. Brown Co., 1972.

5. biologic degradation, 6. competition, 7. habitat, 8. biological niche, 9. range and 10. pollution.

b.   For each term except No. 1 in (a) above, furnish an example with a brief written description.

c.   Select a specific plant species of their choice and list for that plant in its natural habitat:
    1.   the factors enhancing its survival
    2.   the factors working against its survival

d.   Select a specific animal species and treat as in (c) above.

e.   Select a member of the Class Pisces and depict diagrammatically that member's role in the food chain.

f.   Select one agent currently an active pollutant and write an essay describing that agent's role, real and potential, in affecting plant and/or animal life.

Do Objectives Stifle Originality?

A common objection to using objectives is that they encourage, if not demand, the training of humans in a sense that makes them akin to puppets. In other words, everyone is to learn only specific behaviors and hence there is no room for self-discovery, originality, inventiveness or whatever you might wish to call that which is subsumed under the general term "creativity." This criticism of objectives and their use would be valid if and only if: (1) objectives are too specific, (2) objectives are poorly conceived, (3) objectives do not reflect reality, (4) objectives are limited to low-level cognitive behaviors and (5) their role and use is misunderstood. Objectives are not inherently evil—their effects are only detrimental if humans permit them to be! Refer to the example TBO in the paragraph above and note that although the required behaviors are specific (definite or precise), they do, for the most part, allow the learner great leeway in response behavior. This aspect of objectives is referred to as the difference between *open* and *closed* objectives or the difference between "specific behaviors" and "specific, behaviors," where the comma in the latter makes a great deal of difference. A specific behavior called for in a TBO specifies the same (exact) behavior of each learner. At times this state of affairs is desirable and the objective is referred to as a *closed objective*. In general, closed objectives do not allow for originality or variation in response; for some objectives, this would be proper. For example, if the learner is acquiring skill in administering artificial respiration by the "mouth-to-mouth" method, the behaviors expected of each learner are essentially alike. On the other hand, an *open objective* does allow for response variation on the part of learners, as can be seen in the example TBO furnished above.

How Are Objectives Related to Accountability?

The topic of accountability is specially treated later in this book. Accountability and all that it involves is becoming a frequently discussed issue in education. Taxpayers, parents, funding agencies and legislators, to name a few parties, are increasingly interested in some type of proof that education in fact is taking place as educators claim. Are funds well spent? Are third graders learning to read? Are schools really doing what they say they are doing? These questions, and others, are difficult to answer unless: (1) the exact nature of what is to be learned is known and (2) the ways to measure what is learned are also known. Specifying what is to be learned is obviously the role played by objectives. Why not make public the exact nature of what learning and schooling are all about? Why should any educator try to hide or cover up what is being taught, what a class is expected to do at the end of instruction or what Johnny should know and do in April, May or June? It has been the hesitancy of teachers and others or the inability of these same people to describe what learning is that has led non-professionals to wonder if all is well at P.S. 57 or Podunk High. Secrecy, hidden goals, double-talk and generalizations invite criticism. That is exactly where education is now. The answer to these critics is to say frankly and straightforwardly, *"This* (specify the objectives) is what we are doing and here is how we will prove it." If there are things educators can't do, they should frankly and freely admit it. If there are some important things to be learned which are difficult to specify, educators should say so and proceed to do the best they can.

Accountability in education is to be responsible for, able to explain or prove that learning has taken place. Ultimately, this means being responsible for learners in the classroom achieving what they are supposed to achieve as defined by TBOs.

The Uses of Objectives

Objectives can play several roles or serve several functions in competency-based education. In the main, objectives (1) are a written, public record of what is to be learned, (2) serve to communicate to the learner what he is to be able to do at the end of the instructional period, (3) serve to help select appropriate instructional activities and (4) serve to help select valid evaluation activities.

The first use has already been dealt with in terms of accountability. However, equally important is letting students know what is expected of them. Expectations in terms of test behaviors are commonly hidden; in fact, some teachers delight in the fact that students are surprised by final examinations, are shocked on discovering what some test questions are about, or can't answer many questions; they, as teachers, have been able to locate obscure, often trivial, items of information overlooked by pupils; examination time is a "guessing game" loaded with potentially traumatic experiences. By high school level it is common knowledge to both teachers and learners that at least half of the *secret* to *getting an education* is *pysching the prof*, and he who has an *in* or a *strategy* which enables him to somehow-or-other *discover* what it is the teacher wants is the one who gets the "*A.*" This "hide and seek" philosophy permeates most grades beyond the primary school level. With few exceptions, learners must be aware of the exact behaviors expected of them at any evaluation time.

The last two functions of objectives in competency-based education are more indirect or implied in the wording of the objectives. Specifying exact behaviors enables the teacher to select appropriate learning activities or to design and suggest alternative instruction strategies appropriate to the individual learner. For example, assume the objective deals with *understanding short stories.* Notice that no behavior is specified in the three italicized words and that teachers Jones and Smith may interpret *understand* to mean entirely different things, and further that pupils may not guess what either Jones or Smith wants (expects as tomorrow's classroom behavior). Jones may assign short story X—in fact, Jones frequently says only, "Read X for tomorrow" and Smith may do the same. However, when tomorrow comes, Jones expects his pupils (without telling them so) to name the author, tell something about the author's life, to have memorized the date the author was born and to answer a series of randomly selected factual items as presented in story X. Smith, on the other hand, expects his learners to dissect the structure of the short story and to answer such questions as: (1) What is the topic sentence in the opening paragraph? (2) What techniques did the author use to build suspense?, etc. Both Jones' and Smith's classroom expectations may catch the learner unprepared. How much better it would be to inform the learners as to the exact nature of the objectives, such as:

For tomorrow you are to read story X and be prepared to:

1. Identify two examples each of the author's use of the literary techniques of suspense building, dependence, indirect humor, simile, metaphor and imagery.
2. Explain briefly how the story reflects the author's ideas relating to social structure.

Informed, the learners can now proceed to utilize available instructional activities and strategies and methods unique to themselves (study habits and techniques) to prepare for "tomorrow's class." Guessing, busywork, misdirected efforts and other non-efficient activities are eliminated.

Finally, specification of objectives, as in the above paragraph, implies the correct evaluation of the objective. If this objective were to be "tested," it would be only appropriate for both Smith and Jones to require the students to identify two examples of each literary technique as listed (perhaps requiring the learner to name the page and paragraph where each example he has identified is located) and to explain (perhaps in writing) how the story reflects the author's ideas relating to social structure. If common sense is used, there would be no excuse for the teacher to administer a true-false test covering the author's age, date of birth, the name of the hero, etc. If the objective is specified in behavioral terms, as it should be, then the evaluation of the objective is clearly implied and the likelihood of students' achieving it is greatly increased.

Competencies as Standards of Performance

Some educators distinguish between performance-based education and competency-based education, while others use the terms interchangeably. When a distinction is made, it usually involves an interpretation of *performance,* meaning "the presence of a behavior," while *competence* means "the behavior plus some additional standard," which implies performing well. It is one thing to drive a car (perform) and another to drive it competently. In either case, we are dealing with some type of criterion or criteria.

In performance-based education, the act or the behavior itself is one criterion. If additional criteria are added, that is, behaving to some standard, and you desire to think of this as competency-based education, you are welcome to do so. However, such distinctions are really beside the point—the major concern is the criterion or the criteria themselves: whether there is one, more than one, their presence in the objective and the relationship of the criteria to achievement testing.

Many objectives have, in addition to the mere performance level standard, some other standard(s) so that the performance must conform to some degree of restriction such as: without error, within 3 minutes, with 90 percent accuracy, for 20 feet, 19 out of 20, maintained for 10 minutes, within 2 degrees, within .0001 gram, etc. Whether standards or criteria beyond mere performance are necessary in all objectives is questionable. The most logical approach is to have level one (mere performance) in all objectives and then add level two (additional criteria) when it is reasonable to do so. Reasons for level two standards can be readily deduced from real life situations in which the level one performance operates. Perhaps what is being said here is that level one is required and without it you have no objective by definition, but that level two standards are optional in an objective and are present only when appropriate.

Evaluation of Objectives

Competency-based education has created a need to rethink the whole area of achievement testing. Without doubt, a new type of test is needed, and it is generally recognized as a criterion-referenced test. In the section above we dealt briefly with criteria or standards. It is these level one and level two standards that give meaning to the terms *performance* and *competency* and also now to *criterion-referenced tests.* Traditional, or norm-referenced, tests have definite characteristics, formats and functions which do not fulfill the requirements demanded of evaluation in competency-based learning. There is nothing new about the idea that tests are constructed for specific purposes or that there is no such thing as an all-purpose test. In competency-based education, evaluation becomes a task of measuring the attainment, by the learner, of the course objectives. Wishing to make statements or decisions relative to an individual and his behavior repertoire rather than statements or decisions based on comparing individuals on their relative achievement, we need to conceptualize a type of test which will meet the demands of this special purpose. A detailed analysis of criterion testing is the subject of another chapter in this book. It is sufficient to say here that *criterion-referenced tests are a direct outgrowth of terminal behavioral objectives.*

Are Objectives the Answer
to Everything?

Last, but by far not least, is the need to realize that objectives won't answer all prayers for help nor remedy all educational ills. Objectives are merely one way, a means, whereby teachers and learners can attempt to "get a handle" on what is to be learned. Using objectives creates some new problems, as well as helping to alleviate aspects of current valid objectives for learning—a task easier said than done. Developing objectives is also time-consuming; but if properly done, it is more than worthwhile. Also, in working with objectives, one soon discovers that they are much easier to create for levels within the Cognitive and Psychomotor Domain than for the Affective Domain. In fact, there have been, to my knowledge, very few complete, acceptable TBOs developed for any attitudes, interests or appreciations.

Finally, when all is said and done, there also appear to be "things" educators want to accomplish that for one reason or another they either can't or don't want to specify as an objective in behavioral terms. For example, you may wish to have your learners "enjoy the opportunity of visiting a natural history museum." How to express this as an objective with a behavioral description? It probably occurs to you that if you require the learner to write or verbalize an "enjoyment response" you may be doing more harm than good. Many learners, aware of the required behavior, would be striving to respond in a fashion acceptable to the teacher rather than expressing their true feelings. This preoccupation could, if not would, destroy the very thing you intended them to acquire—a feeling of enjoyment. This type of contingency has been met by providing for a type of objective called an *experience objective.* In reality, it is not a type of objective, since we have defined an objective as having a behavioral description. However, for the sake of consistency, this exception to the rule is allowed—and experience objectives serve very useful purposes. Experience objectives are never evaluated in a measurement sense—there is no behavior to measure. The method of evaluating experience objectives is merely to verify that the student has had the experience. It is hard to fit experiences into competency-based learning unless you are flexible enough to deal with them at face value.

In summary, objectives are at the heart of performance- and competency-based learning. Behavioral descriptions aid in all facets of communicating about "what is to be learned" but are of special value in letting learners know the nature and minimum expectancies of what is to be learned. Objectives also serve as the base for devising, selecting and sequencing instructional activities.

Another value, to a competency-based program of education, resides in providing the base on which *competency* can be proven or at least evaluated. In a sense this is saying that they serve as the base for devising and selecting achievement tests. Like all things in life, objectives also have their limitations and weaknesses. Objectives can be poorly conceived, and even if well conceived, misused. Also, not all the good things in life can be reduced to definable behaviors—I would enjoy seeing some good objectives stating what one is *doing* when he or she is compassionate, loving, honest or tolerant, to name a few. Where valid objectives *can* be created, they will be found to be extremely helpful in devising instructional strategies for, and evaluating, competencies.

7

The Student Will
Appreciate Competently...

Mary B. Harbeck

"What do I care what Shakespeare did?" says the ninth grader emerging from third-period English class. "Boy, I hope this is the last book I ever have to read," exclaims a high school senior as he turns in the book report. "Take Intro. Psych. from Brown," counsels a college roommate, "It's an A-cer."

As educators grapple with the problem of describing performance objectives in the affective domain, students are continuing to develop attitudes, interests and values. Because we have taught students to "think for themselves," they expect us to respond to their changes in attitude with some kind of positive action. They are not disturbed by the fact that we are seldom able to describe and measure behaviors related to a value system which society should promote. They are disturbed by the cognitive objectives we present and the atmosphere we provide in which they are to learn.

In the meantime, an increasing amount of effort has been expended in attempting to devise measuring instruments to be used by our students. Work in this area or domain has not, however, been keeping pace with the efforts and production pertaining to the cognitive domain, for several reasons.

David R. Krathwohl, in *Handbook II: Affective Domain* (1964), identifies factors which bear on the way that we deal with

Mary B. Harbeck is an Assistant Director in the Department of Science for the District of Columbia Public Schools. She previously served in the Department of Public Instruction of the Commonwealth of Pennsylvania as the Coordinator of Science and Mathematics.

the affective domain. Achievement testing for other than cognitive information is seldom done by individual teachers or school systems unless an educational research project is underway. Although most teachers look for desirable interests and attitudes in their students, neither the teachers nor the students feel the need for evaluating these types of affective behaviors. Perhaps this is a reflection of the feeling that values and interests are a private, individual matter while cognitive knowledge is a public concern and responsibility.

A reluctance to evaluate students in respect to attitudes and character development also tends to diminish any thought of competency-based evaluation in the affective domain. If a student can exhibit the specified behavior in the cognitive domain, we are willing to infer that he has "learned." If he professes to have "an interest in helping to solve social problems," we do not tend to consider this interest as having been deliberately engendered by the learning situation at hand, and usually no assessment is made of such an interest.

The belief that affective behaviors develop slowly and must be measured on a delayed basis, perhaps years later, makes the evaluation more formidable. As the research into the learning process continues, it may be found that cognitive learning, at least on the higher levels, needs a long period of time also. By watching the shifts in public attitudes about political problems, one might surmise that changes in attitudes and interests can happen in very short periods of time. Perhaps the real situation is that, in both domains, some objectives can be learned and measured quickly and others require long-range, continuing learning and a much-delayed time for measurement.

Evaluation in the Affective Domain

The current push to develop competency-based evaluation is causing a re-examination of the way that the evaluation proceeds in the affective domain. Educators everywhere are attending workshops on how to write behavioral objectives with accompanying criterion-test items. Teachers are learning that it is desirable to set up an instructional system in which all the objectives for every student can be specified in advance and the achievement of each objective can be reliably measured. They are learning how to pretest and posttest so that students can be evaluated and advanced along a continuum of behavior modification. These techniques of curriculum building are helping to facilitate the development of individualized scheduling, self-instructional packages and independent progress programs in schools. These developments seem to offer hope for solving some of the dilemmas in present-day education. Many practitioners are honestly trying to include evaluation of the affective domain in their "model" for instructional systems, but are feeling frustration to the point of paralysis when actually trying to find or prepare objectives and evaluation items. It is difficult to capture in "action words" the internalized attitudes, feelings and values that we want our students to attain. Most educators agree that it is not desirable, nor even possible, to grade students on their accomplishments in the affective domain.

Opposition

The educators who oppose the idea of constructing instructional objectives to be used for "accountability" and other purposes are concerned about the negative effects on students that such a plan might have. H.R. Crane points out that we know very little about how schoolroom experience contributes to developing creativity in students. Investigation of creative thought shows that hard, serious, effort precedes the "flash of genius" which may not come until years later. No one has devised a way to measure inventiveness, let alone develop an instructional sequence or provide a learning situation for it. There is a danger that our efforts to prescribe every step in a student's learning sequence may inhibit the development of whatever creative power he has.

Interim Step

As an interim step in the transition toward measuring achievement of objectives in the affective domain, it may be useful for the teacher to attempt to evaluate the learning environment which is provided for students. If it can be assumed that young people tend to adopt the values and interests held by the adults whom they respect and admire, then teachers have an opportunity and responsibility to exhibit the same interests, enthusiasms and preferences that they wish to inculcate in students.

These questions may be useful in assessing the extent to which the attitudes and values held by an educator are portrayed (hopefully for emulation) to students:

1. How is enthusiasm for the learning exhibited? Science teachers who are doing some research problem of their own can help by sharing it with students. Do your students ever see you reading a journal in your field? Do they know that you attend professional meetings, and that you enjoy going?

2. Are classwork and homework assignments designed to be obviously useful to the student? Are term papers and laboratory reports used for something in addition to earning a grade?

3. Are topics which are supposed to result in an aesthetic experience for students discussed and dissected until all the life is gone out of them? Perhaps works of art, music and literature can be enjoyed without complete understanding of how each component fits into the whole structure. The "life and times" topics in social studies may be more appreciated by students if they are taught with a variety of current and local illustrative material and less lecture and discussion.

4. Is there hope for students who are having difficulty in learning in a particular area of study? When students meet frustration in learning, they need to feel challenged rather than defeated. If the teacher exhibits a feeling that the student will succeed, given more time and help, then the student is less likely to give up the effort to learn. Are individual difficulties diagnosed early so that help can be provided promptly? Do students know that you want them to succeed?

5. Is the student offered more than one way to learn? A poor reader is not likely to value any course in which he must read extensively in order to succeed. Conversely, he is not likely to learn to read and to enjoy reading, unless he has opportunities to gain experiences and values to bring to the printed page. The use of pictures, tapes, television, field trips, outdoor education and

other avenues of learning makes it possible for each student to find a way that is conducive to success for him.

6. Is the work paced slowly enough to allow for reflective thinking? Are discussions based on "open" questions which allow for more than monosyllabic answers and recital of facts? What percentage of the class feels overwhelmed by the amount of material which must be dealt with?

7. Do the students think of the classes as "our" classes or "your" classes? Do they have the opportunity to help in planning how the work is to be done? Do they know you respect each person and value his opinions?

8. Can you laugh with students about your own foibles? Can you enjoy some of their interests with them? Is your classroom atmosphere comfortable and friendly? Do they know that you like them?

9. Do you offer a valid rationale or purpose for the objectives which you want students to reach?

10. Do you enter each class well prepared, so that you are secure enough to allow for flexibility in procedure and can revise your plans to fit any special situation or opportunity which occurs?

Teachers can use these or similar questions to do a self-evaluation or as a basis for student-evaluation of the classroom atmosphere.

Despite the problems connected with evaluation in the affective areas of behavior, the effort cannot be abandoned. This area of thought and feeling is central to producing educated people. Without it the cognitive and psychomotor domains resemble training and do not produce individuals who have their capabilities fully developed.

Clearly Stated Objectives

The first task that teachers must undertake is to state clearly the objectives they wish students to achieve. This is difficult because words like "appreciate," "be interested in" and "be willing to" are open to numerous interpretations.

Sund and Picard (1972) suggest that objectives may be

written for both overt and covert behaviors and that the covert behaviors can be evaluated indirectly by asking the student about his values, appreciations and attitudes. They further suggest that one should begin to write objectives on the valuing level of the affective taxonomy, rather than the lower levels of being aware or being willing to respond.

Let us assume that the affective objectives for a given course are written as clearly as possible. How, then, shall the evaluation be made? Bloom (1971) suggests that the next step is to devise situations and techniques which will allow (not command) the student to perform the desired behaviors. At this point the attention of the evaluator should be on assessing the goals of the curriculum, rather than on evaluating the individual students. If the majority of students in a group do not show the desired behavior, then revisions in the curriculum can be undertaken in an effort to improve the outcomes.

A Continuous Effort

If affective goals are to remain a part of the curriculum, then a continuous effort must be made to evaluate their attainment. Otherwise, instruction designed to foster certain socially desirable objectives will fall into disuse and the curriculum will become more cognitively centered. Affective objectives need not be evaluated on an individual basis. Group data can be collected by using instruments which can be gathered anonymously from students. This helps to keep students from giving answers that they know will be pleasing to the teacher. By adopting this procedure, the teacher can administer various types of instruments without infringing on the student's privacy. However, if a position of trust exists between teacher and students, and papers are signed, then it is possible to counsel privately with individual students about their responses. Students need to be reassured that their known responses will not be reflected in the grades they earn for cognitive learning.

There are several types of instruments being used by teachers to collect group data, such as interview schedules, checklist, open-ended questions, questionnaires with fixed alternatives and semantic differential techniques.

The use of observation and interviewing is time-consuming, but by structuring what behaviors are to be watched for or asked about during an interview it is possible to make inferences about the interests and attitudes of students. A record of an observation can be in the form of a checklist:

.....1. Follows safety rules during lab procedures.

.....2. Records data as he works.

.....3. Cleans glassware at the end of lab.

.....4. Replicates experiment until sufficient data are collected.

Interview data can be collected by planning a few set questions to be included as the opportunity arises in informal conversations with each student.

1. Did you think the procedure we used for collecting water samples last week was adequate?

2. Should the unit on water pollution be used in the class next year?

3. Are you planning to take another biology course?

4. Do your friends ever express a desire to take this course?

Some teachers feel that a written checklist is better than oral interviewing because students feel more free to express opinions honestly on an unsigned paper.

Closed-item questionnaires which resemble highly structured interviews can be prepared. It is thought to be advantageous to have these instruments administered by a neutral person, such as a guidance counselor or a student from another class.

1. The phrase "scientists say" as it is used in advertising should be (a) believed (b) ignored (c) considered (d) disbelieved by the reader.

2. Encircle A, if you enjoy reading non-fiction books. Encircle B, if you enjoy reading books of fiction. Encircle C, if you do not enjoy either fiction or non-fiction.

Open-ended questions can be used to surmise the beliefs and values which students have. If the questions are stated in an impersonal way, the responses may be more honest.

1. If a mining company offers to strip-mine in our area, the

community leaders should . . .

    2. If we win the basketball game, we should celebrate by . . .

    A semantic differential rating scale can be used to evaluate a generalized attitude toward concepts. The student is asked to place a check along a continuum between bipolar adjective pairs. Writing stories in English class is:

useful .... useless
interesting ....boring
easy ....hard
good .... bad
necessary .... unnecessary
exciting .... unexciting
serious.. silly

    By collecting items over a period of time it is possible to build a repertoire of instruments to be used at different times or for different purposes. A good evaluation program for affective objectives evolves as revisions are made and tried out. A variety of items will be needed because of the individuality of students and the many kinds of behaviors being sought. Look for trends in the thinking and feelings of groups, not individual attainments.

    Although the ways of measuring growth in the affective domain are not yet very well understood, some beginnings have been made. The frustrations encountered in this endeavor may well be the challenge that lies in education and makes it the exciting profession that it is.

References

Bloom, Benjamin S., J.T. Hastings and George F. Madaus. *Handbook on Formative and Summative Evaluation of Student Learning.* New York: McGraw-Hill Book Company, 1971, Chapters 10 and 18.

Crane, H.R. A Scientist Looks at Education. *Educational Technology,* January 1970, 22-23.

Eiss, A.F. and M.B. Harbeck. *Behavioral Objectives in the Affective Domain.* Washington, D.C.: National Science Teachers Association, 1969.

Kibler, Robert V., Larry L. Barker and David T. Miles. *Behavioral Objectives and Instruction.* Boston: Allyn and Bacon, 1970.

Krathwohl, David R., B.S. Bloom and B. Masia. *Taxonomy of Educational*

Objectives: Handbook II: Affective Domain. New York: David McKay
    Company, 1964.
Sund, Robert B. and Anthony V. Picard. *Behavioral Objectives and
    Evaluation Measures: Science and Mathematics.* Columbus, Ohio:
    Charles E. Merrill, 1972.

8

Learning Modules for Competency-Based Education

Joe Lars Klingstedt

A learning module (LM) is a type of curriculum package that has been developed to answer a specific need of educators involved with competency-based education. Before we discuss LMs, let's see how the need for them evolved. Professionals in the area of curriculum development, at any level, will generally agree that curriculum may be defined as "a planned series of learning outcomes for which the school is responsible." This is not a new definition, but when it is used in connection with competency-based education it takes on a new meaning. That new meaning is related to a clearer definition of the word "outcomes." Many "outcomes" of the past have been stated in extremely vague terms, i.e., they have not always communicated the intent of the writer or writers. In an effort to solve this problem, an increasing number of curriculum specialists are replacing the vague terms of the past with specific, behavioral objectives. To those involved with competency-based education, specific, behavioral objectives (also called performance objectives) are a must—they must precede all else. Hence, the first step in the development of a competency-based education program is to identify the performance objectives for the program.

Many articles, pamphlets and books have been written to help educators learn what performance objectives are and how to write and use them. As educators across the country became

Joe Lars Klingstedt is Assistant Professor of Curriculum and Instruction at the University of Texas at El Paso.

skilled in identifying outcomes in terms of performance objectives, they began to realize that this was only a first step in the improvement of education as a whole. Something else was needed. Performance objectives solved the problem of the vague "outcomes" of the past, but what could be done to improve the probability of student success? Most teachers have always considered themselves unique persons, but only recently have they begun to be concerned with the uniqueness of their students. With the increased awareness of the value of individualized instruction, many teachers feel that they can no longer continue to "do their own thing" if they wish to reach a more significant number of their students. The LM was developed as a result of this concern. Although it is not a cure-all, it does have much to offer in terms of allowing both the teacher and student to "do their own thing"; and at the same time the LM increases the chances that the learner will accomplish the stated objectives.

Upon completion of this chapter, the reader should be able to: (1) write a brief paragraph describing, from memory, the purpose of a learning module, and (2) list and describe, from memory, the six major parts of a learning module.

Objectives

The paragraph above states the objectives which you, the reader, should be able to accomplish after you have completed this chapter. It is not a coincidence that these objectives were placed at the beginning of the explanation of learning modules because the *first thing* to be included in an LM is the *objective* or objectives to be accomplished. Objectives are the behaviors, or performances, toward which the learner works. In an LM, objectives should always be stated in performance terms, i.e., they should communicate, in specific, behavioral language, exactly what the learner is to be able to do upon completion of the module.

Pretest

The *second part* of the LM is the *pretest*. The function of the pretest is to help the teacher and the learner determine if it is necessary to proceed through the module. If the learner can demonstrate the required competency without completing the module—great! The only reason why a teacher might want a learner to go ahead with a module even after successful completion of the pretest would be for enrichment or reinforcement. Do you need to finish this chapter? Let's see.

State, in writing, the purpose of a learning module. ....
....
....

From the list below, select the six words which best describe the major parts of an LM. In the space provided, indicate the order in which you think they should appear.

..........Seminars   ....Recycling

..........Learning   ....Rationale
         Alternatives

..........Slide-tapes   ....Feedback

..........Individualized   ....Content
                                                    Description

..........Group   ....Directions
         Organization   for Use

..........Film Loops   ....Goal

..........Programmed   ....Performance
         Instruction   Objectives

..........Demonstrations   ....Purpose

..........Measurement   ....Pretest

..........Posttest   ....Study
                                                    Questions

..........Prerequisites   ....Resources

Although you need not have used the same words, your statement of the purpose of an LM should have conveyed the idea that a learning module should individualize instruction so the learner is able to identify the objectives, progress at his own rate in his own learning style, identify his strengths and weaknesses, and recycle when objectives have not been achieved.

Although study questions, flow charts, time requirements, prerequisites, etc., are often included in LMs, the *six major parts* are: (1) *objectives,* (2) *pretest,* (3) *rationale,* (4) *learning alternatives,* (5) *posttest* and (6) *resources.*

If your responses agreed with those given above, you have passed the pretest for this chapter and need not read further (unless, of course, you wish to do so for enrichment or reinforcement).

Constructing pretests, and posttests for that matter, is really an easy task *if* the objectives have been stated in performance terms. As you can see by comparing the pretest above with the objectives stated earlier, test questions are derived from objectives. This is extremely important, because it makes little sense to go through the process of constructing performance objectives unless they are to be utilized in instruction and testing.

Many times, as is the case here, the writer of an LM may wish to provide the learner with information which he can use to check his responses upon completion of the pretest. Whether this information is available to the learner or not, the teacher should have it prepared so that the pretest can be checked immediately.

Rationale

The *third major part* of an LM is the *rationale* section. The sole purpose of the rationale section is to establish the value of the LM. The learner may understand the objectives and still not see how the accomplishment of them will help in any way. The rationale section of the LM should attend to this concern explicitly. It should indicate to the learner how the accomplishment of the stated objectives will be useful to him both now and in the future. Anyone using LMs should make it clear to the learners that if they still do not see the value of a given LM after reading the rationale section they should consult with the teacher before going any farther. It is not enough for the learner to feel that he will see the value of the LM later—by that time, in all likelihood, he will have forgotten what was included in the module.

Learning Alternatives

The *fourth part* of an LM is the section in which the learner is presented with *learning alternatives* which are designed to help him accomplish the objectives of the module. The learning alternatives are really the heart of the LM. They allow the learners to "do their own thing" in terms of how they go about accomplishing the objectives. At the same time, learning alternatives allow teachers to "do their own thing" in terms of instructional style, especially where team teaching is the rule and not the exception.

To see how this works, consider the points mentioned previously about the uniqueness of both teachers and learners. The professional has a style whereas the amateur does not. If we are talking about teachers as professionals, then it would seem logical to assume that each teacher has an instructional style with which he is most comfortable and effective. To force him to quit doing what he does best would not only be unfair to him but to his students also. But what about the learning style of the students? What if the student learns most effectively from audio-visual materials and the teacher's thing happens to be lecturing? Who must change? No one! Through the use of learning alternatives, both options are available. In fact, there are usually several more than these two. The idea is for the teacher to identify the options that seem most likely to allow the learners to progress at their own rate in their own learning style. (Remember the purpose of an LM? It was stated that the purpose of a learning module is to *individualize instruction* so the learner is able to identify the objectives, *progress at his own rate in his own learning style,* identify his strengths and weaknesses and recycle when objectives have not been achieved.) If the teacher identifies four viable alternatives, let's say programmed instruction, lecture-seminar, slide-tape and reading selected material, and if he is a part of a team, he can prepare the option which best fits his instructional style, and other team members can prepare the other options. In this manner the learner has a choice and the teacher gets to utilize his most effective teaching style.

But what if the teacher is not involved in team teaching? Does that mean that he or she cannot use LMs? No, it does not mean that at all. An increasing number of LMs are becoming available with several alternatives already prepared. The teacher may select from these, and in many cases add another option to those included. If there are not any modules available that fill the needs of the teacher and learners, and if the teacher is not involved in team teaching, LMs can still be used on a limited basis.

If the teacher constructs his own modules, he should be able to provide at least two options, and probably more, for the learners. The teacher who happens to find lecturing to be his most effective technique could surely, with a little effort, come up with a worthwhile reading alternative for those learners who just did not tune in on his lectures. In addition, he might be able to find a movie or a slide-tape that would prove useful as a learning alternative for some of his students. Many LMs contain material written especially for the module in an effort to provide a specifically focused reading alternative for the learners. After a few tries, many teachers find that they can do quite well writing their own material for modules.

Posttest

The *fifth part* of an LM is the *posttest.* Like the pretest, the posttest is designed to measure the learner's achievement of the objectives in the module. Although the learners normally complete the LM before taking the posttest, this is not required. The learner may usually take the posttest anytime he feels ready. Questions on the posttest should be derived from the objectives. It is not fair to the learner to indicate in the objectives section what he is to be able to do at the end of the module and then test him on something else.

What if the learner fails to perform up to the required level of competency? He should recycle himself and concentrate on the behaviors he has not acquired. This points out another value of learning alternatives. If the learner selected the lecture-seminar alternative the first time and was unable to follow the main ideas presented, he may go back and select another alternative, say selected readings, that might be more helpful *for him.*

Resources

The *sixth* and final *part* of a learning module is the *resources section.* The resources section is the place where all needed materials, media and readings are listed. Also included in the resources section may be such things as flow charts, time requirements, evaluation forms and the like.

Summary

Learning modules include, but go one step beyond, performance objectives. They provide a way for learners to progress at their own rate in their own learning style, identify their strengths and weaknesses, and recycle when objectives have not been met. They allow for flexibility in terms of instructional and learning styles. Although they may contain many elements, six major parts are usually present—objectives, pretest, rationale, learning alternatives, posttest and resources.

Since competency-based education is concerned with the individual's ability to perform up to a given criterion level, it seems to follow that educators who are involved in the development of competency-based educational programs have an obligation to perform up to a certain level. Surely one responsibility is to develop programs that will increase the probability of learner success. Learning modules may not be the complete answer, but they have demonstrated that they are more successful with many learners than the sole use of the old "spray and pray" lecture technique of the past.

9

A Humanized Model of
Computer Managed Instruction

**J. Bruce Burke, Julia O'Neill
and Kay Welsch**

One of the persistent problems in contemporary education is the difficulty which arises in trying to provide students with the personal attention appropriate to their individual needs while at the same time trying to maintain a system of education that is cost-benefit effective in relation to society's needs and resources. Increasingly, schools and colleges are turning to technology and instructional media in attempts to solve this problem. Faced with rising instructional costs to meet the demands of greater numbers and diversity in the student population, educators see in the tool of computer technology a potentially powerful remedy to relieve the pressures on the budget. Care must be exercised, however, to insure that students are not tracked into programs which do not permit precise assessment of needs nor the flexibility of student decision points. The question, thus, is how a computer managed instructional system can be humanized to let each student follow his own bent, fulfilling his own goals, while providing him with a system of guided learning activities. In this proposal we outline a plan designed to apply to any subject area or learner level. The objective is to individualize a program for the teacher trainer, using a computer for management, but designing student decision loops into the system so that the student does not feel as though he is being run through an assembly line.

J. Bruce Burke is director, Humanities Teaching Institute, College of Education, Michigan State University. **Julia O'Neill** and **Kay Welsch** are instructors, College of Education, Michigan State University.

The Conceptual Model

Several significant concepts are built into this system. The whole program, including the affective learning, is based on the mastery model, with behavioral objectives stated in performance terms, providing built-in evaluation of progress by both student and instructor.

One objection to the mastery model raised by defenders of the grading system is the apparent difficulty in categorizing student ability. According to some, everyone who completes a competency-based program will be labeled only proficient and will not be differentiated between "gifted" and "average" achievers. However, this need not be true if a program has a variety of options. Of course, if a program is mapped out with all modules required, the only indicator of difference would be time: and that would identify only, to some extent, speed of learning. But there are other traits more indicative of educational achievement and these will manifest themselves only if the program is truly individualized, full of options and stimulating fare which allow the student freedom to set his own pattern of content and direction. In that case the truly educated, self-directed, persevering learner will have a much more extensive record of achieved objectives, exemplified by variety, thoroughness and relevance.

The performance objectives are to be sequenced in topic-oriented clusters called modules. Intellectual objectives will emphasize higher levels of learning and also will be selected on the basis of the conceptual model of teaching which strongly influences the total program.

The framework of this system is the conceptual model of teaching adapted from the work of Professor Judy Henderson at Michigan State University.* The two broad categories are instructional design and instruction. Instructional design is the series of tasks carried out by the instructor (who may be the learner himself, since self-instruction is intended learning, as opposed to accidental learning), prior to the implementation of the design.

*See J. Henderson *et al. Education 200 Handbook: The Individual and the School.* East Lansing: M.S.U. Press, 1971.

Under each category the steps of assessing, setting objectives, planning strategies and evaluating meet the criteria of a mastery model. Any one of these steps, omitted or poorly planned, can be a weak spot in an otherwise adequate system. As mentioned earlier, it is strongly recommended that this model of learning apply to the majority of objectives; if done, this actually teaches the relevance as well as content. This might be described more fully as a series of questions one asks when dealing with intellectual and affective material.

> What is going on here? (Assessment: collect data, analyze, hypothesize)
>> 1.   That is, what relevant behavior is observed?
>> 2.   What does it mean?
> What will I do with this data? (Objective)
> How will I do it? (Strategy)
> How will I know if I've succeeded? (Evaluation)

Staffing

To meet the tasks required of the staff to implement this system, differentiated staffing is projected. While the student may do some of the cognitive learning solo, there is a need at the very least for personal attention in the stages of simulation and clinical experience, and in the affective domain. It is very doubtful that many students will learn the connotative meaning of much of the material without extensive interaction with peers and instructors as well as practice. The plan proposes a counselor-instructor who will spend much of his time with students (approximately 75 percent instruction and 25 percent instructional design). He will be directly employed in teacher education and may have the responsibility of guiding students throughout their program. His qualifications should include success as a student counselor, understanding of human behavior, ability to provide growth experiences and a comprehension of the general methods segment of the teacher training program. The complementary role of course instructor would be filled by staff members who were more content-oriented. These instructors, who would design programs primarily (75 percent instructional design) and interact with students concerning specific experiences in their area of specialization (25 percent instruction), could be appointed either to the education staff, or within their own department be designated to provide the courses needed by teacher trainees. In either instance, the most important factor is the ability of this instructor to model the kind of effective teaching that the student is expected to learn. He should also work closely with the counselor-instructor so that he may obtain feedback and have adequate assessment data and not fall into the trap of developing "ivory tower" modules. Also, the counselor-instructor can be kept up-to-date on content and methods so that he doesn't become isolated from the cognitive area. Staff interaction and cooperation is undoubtedly one of the most important elements of a successful program, as it can avert the tribalism toward which many faculty groups tend.

Both types of instructors will be responsible to the team of faculty, whose primary tasks will be coordination of the program. A variety of specialties can be beneficial here, for example, systems analyst, curriculum coordinator, computer programmers, personnel director, clinic supervisor, audio-visual expert, etc. The team of coordinators would be accountable to the administration for student performance, that is, course effectiveness.

One last note before discussing the subsystems of the student program: This model of a teacher education program is a projected goal toward which one can work, but it is doubtful that the funds and personnel would be available to institute it totally from the beginning. With this reality in mind, the ideas can be implemented in a few courses for a starter, as they are at Michigan State University. The trial-and-error approach can help refine many program facets. Later implementation can be expanded to a few courses at a time until it is realistic to apply the model to an overall teacher education program, including all course work the students take while at college. The narrative description of the flowchart suggests the process by which one or more courses may be redesigned into modular form and developed for use on an information retrieval system.

Computer

The most crucial element of computerizing individual instruction is the effort to prevent students from feeling machine-directed. The computer can be effective in storing modules and performance data, but if the student feels arbitrarily manipulated, such efficacy is wasted. The prime problem is how to use the computer for information retrieval, yet give the student a major role in determining his options and direction. The following program, which could be instituted in anything from a single course to a total professional program, seeks to answer the question. In this program the computer will contain all of the modules available to the student, stored in a natural language system, such as the BIRS or APL program. Each module must be coded with the required prerequisite modules, so that only those for which the student has had the prerequisite knowledge will be made available to him. The modules must contain the basic required objectives and optional objectives, a list of alternate strategies for meeting each of those objectives—the materials, methods and milieu available—and a list of resource personnel and information regarding pretesting and posttesting. Other data in the computer will be the bookkeeping of student progress. Each numbered objective which the student masters will be noted on his records. The evaluation of students through the mastery plan makes it possible to list achievement by the notation of the quantity, quality, content and variety of objectives a student masters. The prospective employers can identify the students' capabilities and specialization or diversity of interests, which is what they really want to know. It should be very obvious to one who reads a mastery record what the competency differences are between the student who does the minimum required of him and the student who goes on to sample a number of options available to him in a wide variety of areas.

Another block of data which the computer needs to contain is the availability of instructional milieus. The information would be made available to the student as to when he could participate in a small group discussion, encounter, micro-lab, clinical experience or one-to-one discussion with instructor or counselor, and also

where and with whom.

In the narrative of the system, given below, we describe the progress of a student in a program using this system.

Flowchart

Once a student is accepted into the teacher education curriculum, he begins a self-directed program of study. (See Figure 1.) The only immediate requirement is that he will be assigned to a small group and a counselor-instructor (CI). It might be advantageous to keep this group and instructor together throughout the program.

The first step in the teaching process is to assess where the student is, what his needs and skills are and what the most meaningful direction would be for him. The small group is one place for these to be ascertained. The student should begin with peers to develop an understanding of a conceptual model of teaching and learning and his roles in relation to that model. This should give him a framework on which to begin building his competencies as a teacher. He should look at himself and his relationships with people. Both of these processes, if handled well, should do more to motivate the students (by helping them to identify their own cognitive and affective skills) than most of the usual artificial means educators have thus far formulated, e.g., grades, required courses. A third factor in motivation would be placement in the real world of the classroom very early in his program, beginning as an observer, rapidly moving to aide and then practice instructor. In this model there is also the opportunity for one-to-one contact with the counselor-instructor where there is need, rather than sending the student to a more distant counseling center, since this aspect of self-knowledge and self-growth, as well as academic guidance, is an integral part of the program. We suggest that this procedure does not work in a program where instructors are seen as judgmental, authoritative and superior. The instructor must be perceived as the significant person who provides the guidance to help the student grow and learn. Especially when the student bogs down on his own, the counselor-instructor is seen as a person with a vested interest in

Figure 1

Instructional System Flow Chart

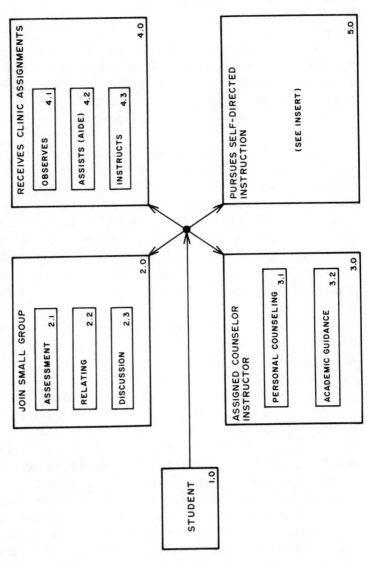

Figure 2a

Student Pursues Self-Directed Instruction

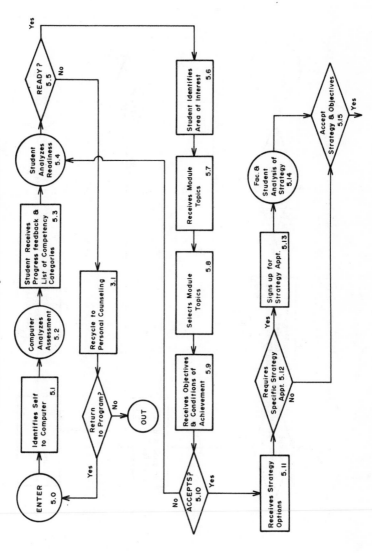

Figure 2b

Student Pursues Self-Directed Instruction

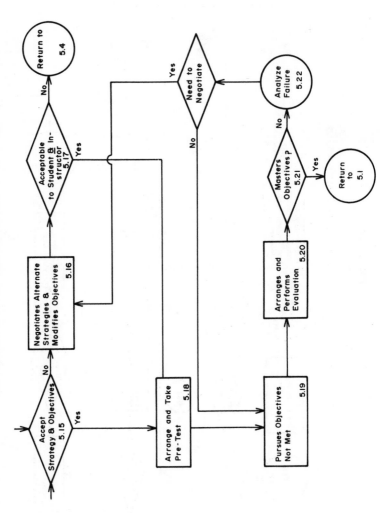

the student's mastery of relevant skills for facilitating growth in self and others.

As the student prepares to learn new skills, he will be ready to look at some of the objectives in the program. There will be a basic core of objectives, identified as probably desirable for teachers to meet, not just cognitive, but affective as well—such as the teaching of reading and the ability to relate to people—and a wide variety of options which the student will select as they become relevant to him.

The key feature of the process of self-directed instruction designed into this program is the student decision loops by which instructional flexibility results from student analysis of his own progress. Let us assume a student has been prepared to enter and to use the computer "library" by his counselor-instructor and small group experiences. (See Figures 2a and 2b.) The student identifies himself to the computer, feeding into the records any additional relevant data about himself that the computer may not have (5.1). The computer analyzes the assessment data (5.2) and reports to the student a profile of his progress to date and lists the competency categories the student has yet to complete (5.3). The student has the opportunity at this point to analyze his own readiness to proceed with the instructional activities (5.4). It is important for the student to assess his own progress and make a decision as to his readiness to continue at any point in time (5.5). If the student decides against continuing at this point, it may be because he feels a need for further discussions with his counselor-instructor to sort out his analysis. Is he really committed to teaching? Does he understand what his opportunities are? Should he do something else to prepare for this instruction proposed? These and other questions should be raised in the counseling session (3.1). If the student is not ready, he leaves the program, either on a temporary or permanent basis. If he is ready, he can automatically return to the program.

The student identifies his area of interest, e.g., psychology (5.6), and the computer replies with a list of the specific module topics (5.7), e.g., Piaget's principles applied to education for which the student has demonstrated the prerequisite skills. (The computer contains a record of his progress.) The student selects the module topic he thinks he is most interested in, and advises the computer of his choice (5.8), to which the computer responds by listing the objectives and conditions of achievement within the module (5.9).

At this point the student has three options. He may decide that he is not interested or ready to pursue the module; so he returns to the decision point (5.4) to analyze his readiness anew and proceed to select another module or recycle to counseling. He may decide he wants to pursue the objectives as given, or he may like some of the objectives but not all. In the last two situations he asks for the strategy options (5.11). The computer gives the strategy information, which includes helpful materials such as audio-visual aids, books, resource instructors, lectures or groups to attend. With this information in hand, the student asks himself whether or not he understands the requirements and the variety of means to meet them. If he has any doubts, he schedules a strategy appointment (5.12, 5.13). The student meets with an instructor to analyze the strategy options (5.14).

If the student is satisfied with the objectives and strategies he proceeds directly to take the pretest (5.18) and arranges for pursuing those objectives not met by pretesting (5.19). If, however, the student is not satisfied with the objectives and strategies as outlined, he then has the opportunity to negotiate (5.16) with the counselor-instructor or perhaps a subject-instructor alternative objectives and strategies acceptable to both (5.17). If the negotiation process breaks down, the student returns to the point of readiness analysis (5.4) and either chooses another module or seeks further counseling. The negotiation process is essential to the system in order to assure student perception of the relevance of his instructional experiences. The degree of participation in planning one's own activities is a measure of one's responsibility for what is learned. We cannot expect the products of education to exhibit responsible behaviors unless there are opportunities to practice such responsibility. We are, of course, also concerned that students have a balanced program and adequate base of information; but students can come to see the unfavorable consequences of consistently avoiding difficult activities or uninteresting material, if the avoidance really stunts the development of desired competencies.

When a satisfactory negotiation is arranged, the student then proceeds to pretest and pursue objectives (5.19). All students are expected to decide when they are ready for evaluation (5.20). The computer modules suggest several evaluative methods, from which the student may now choose, e.g., written, oral, clinic performance. He either contacts the instructor or tells the computer to make the arrangements, whichever the module design suggests. When the student has achieved mastery of the objectives (5.21), the instructor gives this information to the computer, which then ejects that module from that student's program and adds others for which it was prerequisite. The student then is ready to come back to the computer for further instructional information.

If the student fails to meet mastery level, this is viewed as an opportunity to analyze his failure (5.22). Was the failure a result of need for more practice? If so, he returns to pursue the objective not met. Perhaps it was that the student set unreasonable demands upon himself and needs to renegotiate the instruction (5.23). No matter what the reason, failure to meet the mastery criteria is not viewed as a taint on the student's permanent record, but an occasion for reassessment and redoubled effort. Soon students learn to accept time as the variable of learning and seek achievement of performance skills as the constant of learning.

Concurrently with this ongoing self-instructional process, the student would be meeting in small groups, with his CI, discussing the meaning of his learning—his reactions to it. He would also be engaged in observing real classes for the purpose of identifying the relevance of his learning. We suggest that if such a plan were followed the result would be that students will not feel dehumanized by an insensitive, unresponsive, mechanistic technology, but will exhibit the freedom that comes with competence and autonomy.

10

Elementary Curriculum Design
for the Future

A competency-based curriculum, if it is to be functional, demands a basis of continuous progress education. For some time professionals concerned with elementary education have professed a commitment to continuous progress education, yet school systems have generally maintained a graded organizational pattern. The outmoded pattern of gradedness and secondary school expectations of achievement have been roadblocks in the attainment of a true continuous progress elementary program. Other inhibiting factors have been the paucity of teachers who can and will diagnose in order to place students on a realistic level for instruction, and also an absence of a systematic program of evaluation to see if the students have attained a level of competence acceptable for placement at another level. It can be assumed that if a competency-based curriculum is to be established, a change in student grading and placement must become a reality.

The traditional methods of curriculum design at the elementary level should also undergo change. Tyler's classic rationale, which has been the basis for so much of the curriculum development of the past two decades, is no longer relevant in selecting curriculum content, as the components of the model themselves have changed. We can no longer turn to the "community" as a source for content selection, as many of today's "communities" are a multiplicity of communities in a constant

Elmer C. Ellis is Professor of Education at Texas Tech University, Lubbock.

state of flux brought on by both mobility and multiple segments with diverse interests and goals. Urbanization renders the identification of community needs almost undefinable—and even by the time they are identified, they probably have changed. Thus, content selected for today's curriculum is often outmoded or irrelevant by the time it is implemented. Curriculum developers would serve the student better by focusing their planning on process as content, choosing experiences which will enhance the student's ability to cope with his rapidly changing environment.

Designers who wish to develop a competency-based curriculum program must define the objectives with a great deal more specificity than has been the case in time past. Not only do we need to know if the program is successful but to what degree, this being the basis for accountability. Woodruff has raised questions with reference to the art curriculum which seem especially appropriate to a competency-based elementary curriculum design. He suggests this process:

1. What behaviors are we trying to produce, in whom and how much?
2. For each of these behaviors, how much of it is conceptual, how much is verbal and how much is motor?
3. What has to be put into the learner to operate as a mediating variable that can and will produce that behavior?
4. What kind of teaching material has the logistic capability of developing it?
5. What do those elements of teaching material look like in a subject matter field?
6. How does a teacher use them to bring about the formation of the mediating variables?
7. How should the materials be programmed for the most efficient input?

The behaviors which are the concern of Woodruff are synonymous with the competencies which are under examination and consideration today.

All this implies the need for an engineering model in which

the product is defined and specifications are given. In other words, what is the job that is to be done? The second dimension of this model will be design strategies for developing the defined product.

In a competency-based elementary curriculum design this means that the selected objectives must be specific and few in number. We need a manageable focus to our subject matter.

Implementation of a
Competency-Based Elementary Curriculum

The question of implementing a competency-based curriculum is one which must be faced. Since the success of any design rests with the teachers who implement it, and as there are many teachers who admittedly do not understand the underlying plan of that which they teach, one would assume that we must develop viable competency-based teacher education programs, both pre-service and inservice.

Change in the present curriculum will come only when teachers become dissatisfied with the curriculum they now have and the ways they are now teaching. Undoubtedly there is much dissatisfaction among teachers as well as administrators and parents with the present curricula in most places. However, teachers who are dissatisfied with what they are doing with children will change only when they know how to do differently. Teacher competencies, although an essential prerequisite if meaningful curriculum designs are to be implemented, are not the subject of this chapter, and are discussed elsewhere. However, consideration has to be given to this topic in order to present a realistic overview of the elementary curriculum.

Projection into the Future

In looking toward the future we may expect the following factors to be influential in elementary curriculum design:

1. Teaching in the elementary school will turn to modularized instructional strategies in which even more emphasis will be placed on individualization of instruction.

2. Teachers prepared in performance-based teacher educa-

tion programs will not be comfortable using the same teaching strategies as the average teacher now utilizes.

3. There will be a greater emphasis on diagnosis in instruction with emphasis upon use of current data.

4. Curriculum in the elementary school will be more sequential than it now is; learning skills in any subject can be diagnosed and pinpointed on the continuum scale.

5. Teachers will more readily utilize varied materials to meet the characteristics in identified subject continuum. All media forms will finally be used and we will finally break away from the textbook curriculum.

6. Textbooks may become "cook book" type, i.e., activity book to implement identified characteristics in the continuum. The elaborate, expensive textbooks which are out of date before they are published will virtually disappear.

7. Teachers will understand the basis for curricular decision-making and will become effective mediators of learning. Not only will teachers know learning theory but will be able to apply this with learners.

Problems in Future Curriculum Design

In developing a competency-based curriculum, each school system must take a close look at its philosophy of education, and the individual practitioner must examine his philosophy in relation to the total school's philosophy. What do we believe education should do for the person and for society? What kind of competencies will the student need in order to be this kind of person? Will he be prepared to operate in a society not yet visualized? With the tremendous changes which are engulfing us, we know that the effective person of the future will be one who can change directions quickly and often. He must be adaptable, flexible, and know how to learn. This means that we must seek new approaches to ways of developing this kind of adult as well as making more effective use of proven methods and techniques. For example, reinforcement theory has been with us for a long time, yet we find relatively few teachers using it to help the child develop the kinds of behavior that he needs in order to function effectively in this or future societies.

Whatever form the competency-based elementary curriculum of the future takes, we may be reassured it will be dynamic—for never again will we be allowed the questionable luxury of a static, outmoded curriculum of the kind with which we are so familiar.

References

Tyler, Ralph, W. *Basic Principles of Curriculum and Instruction.* Chicago: The University of Chicago Press, 1949.

Woodruff, Asahel D. *The Examined Curriculum: A Seminar in Art Education for Research and Curriculum Development.* University Park, Pennsylvania: The Pennsylvania State University, 1960.

11

Secondary Curriculum Design
and Competency-Based Education

Horace E. Aubertine

For the better part of the past two decades, perceptive educators have been aware of a gap between the educational needs of students and the curricular requirements of public secondary schools. In a concerted endeavor to ameliorate secondary education, they have reevaluated the intellectual underpinnings of curricula, revised existing courses of study and designed new instructional programs. At times, misdirected effort and zealousness for change per se have resulted in curricula that are rather like dog-and-pony shows, entertaining but not scholastically educational. Other new programs are proving remarkably effective. But in the majority of public secondary schools, despite advances in theory, technique and program design, curricula remain fixed, circumscribed by traditions rooted in an era which no longer exists.

The traditional curriculum maintains as its center or core the intellectual disciplines. Although related disciplines are integrated at times for presentation as a unit, they generally and habitually are regarded as separate entities. They are fused in that they share three broad educational objectives: (1) to transmit scholastic information, (2) to achieve adequate demonstration that facts and concepts are understood and (3) to promote application of learned material in specific ways. These objectives are locked into the basic premise that education is essentially the acquisition of a

Horace E. Aubertine is Coordinator of Teacher Education at Illinois State University, Normal.

body of information which it is the school's primary function to dispense and the student's primary function to acquire—a premise, that is now too limited in scope.

Today's adolescent soon will be responsible not only for his individual productivity and performance, but also for determining the direction taken by and the quality of a society now turbulent and troubled. He will grapple with moral and economic issues engendered by the nation's precipitous entrance into an era of technology, as well as problems fomenting for decades and requiring immediate resolution. He understands, with a sophistication for which he is not sufficiently credited, that, in the dictum of John Dewey, what society needs and demands are citizens who are problem-solvers, and who can cope with their day-to-day world with rational and thoughtful behavior. It seems advisable, then, that the educational experience emphasize intellectual competency, and it is evident that a germane curriculum would be based on the premise that what is of primary import is not acquisition and storage of a body of information, but rather acquisition and application of intellectual skills.

Whatever the future curricular design, the essential conditions should be that study of logical thinking and communication is included and that the program stress pupil performance-toward-competency in intellectual skills.

Teachers in a competency-based pupil education program must be graduates of competency-based teacher education programs, in order to have the practical experience to implement this instructional system and to understand the procedures leading to achievement of objectives. Heretofore, teachers have directed instruction to include specified subject matter and to conform to broad educational objectives. But in a competency-based program their role will alter markedly. Teachers no longer will be primarily dispensers of information and sole evaluators of student achievement; they will have to examine the relationship between information and competency objectives, organize and manage information so that it complies with objectives, and, at the same time, ascertain the validity of the objectives. These functions demand, in turn, a feedback system which will enable teachers to assess program effectiveness under operation (formative evaluation) and, consequently, to make curricular decisions based upon data retrieved.

Varied Instructional Media

Most experienced instructors have developed a style of teaching which relies heavily upon one or two teaching techniques, such as lecture and discussion or question and answer. In the competency program, teachers must be familiar with and adopt more pupil-to-pupil centered instructional modules.

Video and audio tapes are instructional modules when they exhibit or describe tasks involving certain skills and procedures and achieving certain objectives, and when they include information on previous experience required of students to understand the demonstrations and posttests to be administered by the teacher. For example, a video tape could demonstrate the steps in the programming of a computer or the procedures of a chemical experiment and be accompanied by tests students are to take after the tape is finished. Or an audio tape could tell an instructional story about historical events. The tapes themselves are the resources. Tapes can be used to record student performance in the classroom, as well, and be played back, thus serving as feedback systems for both students and teachers.

Teachers and pupils work together toward student attainment of specified competencies; both, then, should participate in assessing the success of student endeavors. The pupils would be advised in advance of the competencies they must achieve before proceeding further in study, and they should be made aware that evaluation of performance is intended to be a diagnostic technique rather than a grading system. Probably, assessment profiles would be the most effective as their broad base and flexibility are suitable to evaluation of competency level achievement. Furthermore, the use of profiles discourages teachers from assuming that performance necessarily leads to proficiency. A group of profiles can be evidence, as well, that a program has ceased to be efficacious or that there are discrepancies in the design.

Working within a competency-based program with specified

objectives and performance assessment procedures, teachers are accountable for their part in the instructional process. They should be specialists in their field and have extensive experience and education not only in teaching techniques, but also in curricular design and evaluation. Moreover, they should be adaptable in working with colleagues not only within their particular subject disciplines but across disciplines as well, for this kind of education calls for an interdisciplinary approach.

Students, too, are accountable for their part in the educational process. By requiring participation and performance, the competency-based program challenges students and, ideally, will serve to dispel that apathy which leads to education being indifferently received and quickly forgotten. Furthermore, this type of education is eminently suited to negating cultural biases, as it can overcome in great part differences due to diverse ethnic backgrounds or environments.

Mandatory today is education which involves students and encourages, through achievement, intellectual competency, a sense of self-identity and the ability to be self-determining. The secondary school must offer this kind of education, and the competency-based curriculum stressing logical thinking and effective use of language can prove a sturdy foundation for educational experience, valid and germane.

12

Achievement Testing in Competency-Based Education

Richard W. Burns

An important function of any learning system is the evaluation of the learning produced by that system. In most traditional classrooms, rightly or wrongly, the burden of this assessment has rested squarely on the teacher, and in fact many teachers view "testing and grading" as a *right* with which they brook no interference. In competency-based education, evaluation may be, in some respects, more vital to the system than in traditional teaching-learning situations. It is the purpose of this chapter to assess the exact role that achievement testing plays in any competency- or performance-based learning.

Competency-based education generally has derived its distinction from the fact that its outcomes are defined in behavioral terms, as objectives with performance standards. Inherent in specific behavioral objectives, if properly developed, are one or more ways to assess the attainment of the objective. *Objectives describing a behavior, but without additional criteria, lead to performance-based education; while behavioral objectives with performance criteria lead to competency-based education.* In measurement terms, attainment of behaviors is accomplished through using either norm-referenced tests (NRT) or criterion-referenced tests (CRT) as described by Glaser (1963). NRTs are applicable to competency-based education only when comparative statements among learners are being made. Although NRTs are

Richard W. Burns is Professor of Education at the University of Texas at El Paso.

generally familiar tools whose structure, characteristics and functioning are quite well established and understood, the same cannot
be said of CRTs (Glaser, 1963). In other words, NRTs have been
the traditional measures of achievement, with their theoretical
structure and use derived primarily from principles established in
psychological test theory. To utilize these same principles for
designing CRTs is questionable, if not impossible (Cronbach and
Gleser, 1965). The need for tests other than NRT has been
perceived (Flanagan, 1951 and Ebel, 1962) for a number of years.
The use of CRT has not followed the need for such measures.
Exactly why this is so is not clear.

Why do we bother with measuring achievement at all? If
human learning is the acquiring, deleting or changing of modifiable
human traits, why not just let these changes occur and then "go
about our business"? This is possible and correct unless you desire
to make statements about or decisions concerning the *individuals*
who learn or the *instructional process* which led to the learning.
Desiring to make statements of either kind based on objective
evidence causes one to measure one or more traits.

Basically there are two ways to get at either the quantitative
or qualitative behaviors of individuals. We can describe such
measurement by either statements concerning the degree of
attainment according to some defined standards, a criterion-reference, or by statements concerning the relative behavior of two or
more individuals from some defined population, a norm-reference.
Whether the trait can be measured directly or indirectly is a moot
point, but as used here if the trait of interest is describable
directly, i.e., the trait is evidenced by an overt behavior, we can
consider it a direct measure. For example, the trait of *high
jumping* is evidenced by high jumping ability and can be
considered to be directly measurable. On the other hand, some
vast numbers of human traits in which we might be interested are
covert. In fact, such traits often exist only as constructs, in which
case the trait is measured indirectly by making observations about
one or more secondary overt behaviors which we can by
agreement decide will indicate or prove the existence of the
covert, primary trait. Adding, generalizing, estimating and tolerat-

ing are specific examples of covert behaviors which may be named in terminal behavioral objectives as primary behaviors to be learned but which must be measured by observing one or more related secondary behaviors.

Any measurement device is a prescribed situation, concerning one or more traits, in which the testee (learner) is placed, and the situation so contrived that the testee cannot attempt or complete the prescription(s) without giving evidence concerning the trait in which the testor is interested. Whether or not the contrived situation (test) does what it is intended to do depends upon several factors, such as: the skills of the test constructor, whether the trait is overt or covert, whether the secondary behavior is a correlate of the primary behavior, the types of behaviors acquired or reinforced during the preparation to answer the test items and the perception of the task by the testee. As a result of observing the examinee in the contrived situation, some objective or relatively objective evidence should be definable and reportable. Reporting undefined scores, marks or measures leads nowhere. The meaning of scores is derived from their exact definition.

In NRT, scores are generally reported as ranks, percentile ranks, age levels, grade levels, curved scores, deciles, etc. In criterion-referenced testing, scores are generally reported as attainment or non-attainment of a prescribed level of behavior or the attainment of a variety of levels and reported as a unit on a continuous, rigidly defined and accepted measurement scale, or possibly as the attainment of a level described and reported as a unit on an arbitrarily defined scale (this would often include the number of percent success scores).

What is meant by the term "criteria"? Branson (1970) refers to adequate criteria as:

> ... behaviors such that independent observers can identify the presence, absence or degree of the pre-scribed behavior in the target population using appro-priate measuring devices. Adequate criterion behavior can be described in terms of a subject matter or a coordinated skill.

This approach, of defining criteria in terms of the mere presence of a behavior, takes some meaning from the distinction between performance-based education and competency-based education where "criteria" means *performance to some standard*. Discussions of criterion-referenced tests will not get far if the term "criteria" has no acceptable meaning. The term "criteria" could imply some *standard* of performance rather than the mere presence of a performance. To simplify this point we could, and perhaps should, think of two levels of criteria. Level I is the presence or absence of a behavior while Level II specifies additional criteria to which the behavior must conform. In this case we don't need to distinguish between performance or competency and a CRT could apply in either case.

A further point has been made by Garvin (Popham, ed., 1971) that criteria, to be criteria, must be relevant. He states:

> Unless at least one of the instructional objectives of a unit envisions a task that must subsequently be performed at a specified level of competence in at least some situation, CRM (*criterion-referenced measurement*) is irrelevant because there *is no* criterion. In this sense, the entire sequence of "social studies" provides no meaningful criterion except, possibly, the entry level for certain "honors courses."

In another sense, some criteria may be entirely or to some degree arbitrary, nonrelevant or meaningless. Even if criteria do not always have a 1:1 relationship with all aspects of that trait in real life, having some is better than having none.

In metric situations the concept of criteria being true *standards* is fairly straightforward. In high jumping, broad jumping, strength of grip measurement, speed of typing and the specification of tolerance limits for a skill or product production, metric measures can be applied. In these instances performance in a quantitative sense has meaning. A twenty-foot broad jumper by definition jumps twice as far as a ten-foot broad jumper.

In non-metric situations some testors conceive of the test itself as the criterion, regardless of what it measures. In this sense the criterion becomes an arbitrary standard of performance, but it is doubtful if its validity can ever be completely understood. For example, let's take a 100 item, multiple choice, history test for consideration. Let's further assume that history is being learned in terms of some citizenship goal. A standard of performance such as 80 percent of the items could be specified as a minimum criterion and the test treated as a CRT. The complexity of the problem at this point can be illustrated by the following statements, each of which I believe to be true.

1. The test could be shown to have logical topical content validity or face validity. (All the items might have been selected by experts who believe the content of the items to be important.)

2. The test could be shown to have some type of logical psychological content validity. (Interviews with examinees indicate that the items measure something beyond mere recall of factual information.)

3. The test could be valid in the sense that it can be shown by concurrent validation to correlate highly with some recognized test of history. (In the final analysis, however, this merely proves that the test in question measures something in common with whatever the validating criterion test measured, which may or may not be history.)

4. It can be logically argued that what the test measures is not history or citizenship but rather the behaviors acquired or reinforced during the learner's learning process. (That is, any particular response an examinee makes to any given item, whether the response is rote memory or abstract reasoning, is undoubtedly more a function of the examinee's learning than it is of the phrasing of the item.)

5. We still have no idea if the test behavior relates to citizenship and it is improbable that such information will ever be acquired.

6. If we could find a way to positively correlate the test with being a good citizen we still wouldn't know if there was any direct causal relationship. It could be argued that perhaps the motivation, concentration and test-

taking habits of the examinees were the same traits that
led to their being good citizens rather than any
knowledge of history.

Because it is possible to make the above statements, it is hard to
conceive of the history test itself (and all situations it represents)
as a true criterion test in the sense that the term "criterion" is
generally used.

On the other hand, an arbitrarily defined classroom achievement test may be a criterion test from a viewpoint not generally
held at this time. Shoemaker (1971) points out that items on a
test (such as a history test) are a subset of a large population of
items which could be on the test; in such a case, a proportion
correct score would be meaningful to the degree that the items
selected for the test constituted a random or stratified-random
sample from the test population. Further, he points out that since
the content population is usually not completely specified and
random sampling is neglected, the proportion correct score
frequently would be meaningless. Shoemaker's analysis would be
true if one, first, accepted the assumption that a group of test
items, as history, represents history, and then, second, applied
traditional psychological test theory to the problem. Shoemaker is
saying it is necessary in achievement testing to be able to
generalize about test results. That is, the test should be an entry
ticket enabling one to make remarks on the basis of test scores to
the population (as history) from which the items were drawn. I do
not believe this viewpoint is applicable to criterion testing. Any
given set of criterion test items, as will be explained later,
measures the interaction of learner and the learning environment
rather than being a random sample of some population of items.
To use a CRT and accompanying proportion correct score as an
instrument for assessing achievement in a criterion sense, the
population of things to be learned would need to be specified, and
each one of them would need to be measured by the criterion
instrument.

Let's first think about what a test of 100 history items
represents. Are the test items merely measures of information or
are they additionally *measures of the instructional processes by*

which the information is gained? It appears that any cognitive test is as much, if not more, a measure of how the cognitive information is gained as it is of the information requested by the test items. If this argument is true, then items reflecting the *instruction* are valid for the instructional process.

Further, if instructional processes reflect some end point—some broad goal—then each subject matter test over a given segment of instruction can be conceived as a small and related segment of that goal. This goal could be what is meant by "an education," "wide-range achievement," "total achievement," "what one learns" or perhaps even "intelligence." Such goals, as listed, are easily perceived as being composed of many subsets of achievement or intellectual factors. This type of reasoning is reflected in the concept of factor analysis.

For example, assuming the goal is expressed as "total achievement" we can then think of the subsets as, in common parlance, history, mathematics, reading, physics, chemistry, etc. Tests can be made of these subsets called *achievement tests* and at this point we are approaching what a common classroom (teacher-made) achievement test is. These subsets of achievement can be thought of as related to the global concept of "total achievement."

Total achievement is not a defined population of elements nor represented by a finite number of test items; but rather, total achievement varies from individual to individual. In any given culture many individuals will achieve common elements and it is these common elements that are measures in our so-called "wide-range achievement tests," as for instance, the *California Achievement Test, SRA* and *Metropolitan.* Analogous to this reasoning is the global concept of scholastic aptitude which is measured by such instruments as the GRE, SAT and ACT.

Now, to return to our original point that tests are as much if not more a measure of the instructional process or method of learning as of information learned, we can see that test information reflects processes such as analyzing, synthesizing, classifying, perceiving, remembering, abstracting, discriminating, conceptualizing, evaluating, translating, creating, estimating, predicting, associating, measuring and theorizing. Additionally, habit patterns and strategies which utilize processes as in problem-solving—call them study habits, problem-solving methods, inductive methods, deductive methods or whatever you wish—are also reflected in achievement tests. It is highly probable that wide-range achievement tests are effective as predictors of past and future learning not because of the cognitive information demanded by the test items, but rather because they reflect, in some global way, the total instructional process. That is, if John or Mary can learn and have learned, if they command the learning or thinking processes, or if they have found study habits that work for them and if they can solve problems it is likely that *they can supply the cognitive information called for by the test.* The effectiveness of the test *does not* depend on the cognitive information itself, but rather on the interaction by which the cognitive information was gained. Any other subset of cognitive items from the same topic would serve equally well. If subsets of achievement are related to "total achievement," the scores on achievement tests are related directly to the learning process. More important, however, is the fact that *in criterion testing a proportion correct score would reflect the individual's command of the learning process.* That is, a score of 20 would reflect less response to the instruction than would a score of 30 or 40. In this sense the achievement test could be conceived as a scale and could be used as a standard of performance, in fact, as a CRT. What then is a criterion-referenced test?

> *A CRT is a measure of the degree of the effectiveness of the interaction between the elements of instruction, the strategy presented for learning and the learning style and ability of the learner.*

In practice, multiple-item verbal tests (true-false, multiple choice, completion, short answer and similar formats) in which each item is to be related directly to measuring a competency as defined in a terminal behavioral objective, are of limited use in CRT. However, since a CRT is a measure of interaction between learner and other learning elements, it is possible to conceive of a multiple-item measuring instrument as a structuring device for an instructional sequence. That is, the multiple items could be formulated and sequenced as an integral part of the instruction process (the means) and further serve as a guide of the direction of behavior development. This type of application is akin to the use of test items in TEST (terminal evaluation structured teaching) methodology and also similar to the use of questions (test items?) in programs of CAI (computer assisted instruction). In this sense, key items (those considered important) could serve as selected members of the total sequence, as a criterion-referenced posttest, in which case 100 percent mastery would be required before the learner was allowed to proceed to the next instructional sequence. The 100 percent mastery would *prove the interaction.*

One could also hypothesize another instance where a multiple-item test could be used as a CRT. This use is similar to, but not quite the same as, our previous history illustration. In this case, the test would be clearly related to the wording or intent of a terminal behavioral objective:

TBO: Learner is to know the 80 items of information as specified on Handout V, so that he can respond in writing to 90 percent of the 80 items requiring recall of the information.

(Note: This is far from an ideal objective and it obviously requires a low-level behavior, assuming there is a hierarchy of behaviors; however, it could be found in reality.)

To measure the above TBO, 80 questions are devised and the test used as a CRT. The validity of this test would simply be a matter of showing face validity or a 1:1 relationship between information items and test items. Such a test *would not* in the NRT sense be considered as an entry ticket to make inferences about "knowledge of history," nor could one imply that if a learner achieved 72 items he knew 90 percent of history. One could use this test only as a criterion-reference in that it indicates some degree of comprehension of the 80 specified items of information and only these 80 items.

A large number of CRTs consist of product and process types of measures rather than verbal types of items. Verbal items are useful in appraising acquisition of factual information, theory and verbal skills while product and process measures are useful in measuring motor skills, habit patterns, thought patterns and mental processes.

Processes and products are easily perceived as applicable in evaluating behaviors as typing, radio repairing, cabinet making, flying, swimming and a thousand other similar behaviors. They are equally applicable to evaluating decision-making, chemistry, literature and other areas where a motor component may not be obvious. Sales ability can be measured best by requiring the trainee to sell. Teaching ability can be evaluated best by observing trainees teach a live group of learners. Chemistry skills can be observed by placing learners in situations exactly like those in which chemists are expected to perform. Chemistry learners can be required to analyze and synthesize real products. The ability to appraise, critique, interpret or summarize novels or poems should be evaluated by requiring the learner to produce a product—an appraisal, a critique, an interpretation or a summary. The concept here is clearly that of placing the learner in a contrived situation that is real or as nearly "life-like" as possible and requiring him to perform (process) or produce (product).

When the method or way of performing (behaving) is important, a process measuring situation is devised and each situation can be thought of as a test item. If the end result is more important than the method, a product measuring situation is required. Products can include plans, blueprints, drawings, paintings, tables, charts, diagrams, models, photographs, collections, specimens, stories, poems and an infinite number of other real things. In many instances much can be inferred about a process from observing a product; the two are interrelated. Evaluations using processes and products are commonly more valid than merely testing at the verbal level, which may or may not indicate competence.

References

Branson, Robert K. The Criterion Problem in Programmed Instruction. *Educational Technology,* July 1970, 35-37.

Cronbach, L.J. and G.C. Gleser. *Psychological Tests and Personnel Decisions.* Urbana, Illinois: University of Illinois Press, 1965.

Ebel, Robert L. Content Standard Test Scores. *Educational and Psychological Measurement,* 1962, 15-25.

Flanagan, J.C. Units Scores and Norms. In E.T. Lindquist (Ed.) *Educational Measurement.* American Council on Education: Washington D.C., 1951, 695-763.

Garvin, Alfred D. The Applicability of Criterion-Referenced Measurement by Content Area and Level. In W.J. Popham (Ed.) *Criterion-Referenecd Measurement.* Englewood Cliffs, N.J.: Educational Technology Publications, 1971, 55-63.

Glaser, Robert. Instructional Technology and the Measurement of Learning Outcomes. *American Psychologist,* 1963, 519-521.

Shoemaker, David M. Criterion-Referenced Measurement Revisited. *Educational Technology,* March 1971, 61-62.

13

Certification Issues in Competency-Based Teacher Education

Theodore E. Andrews

My friends tell me that I often confuse competency-based teacher education and competency-based certification: that the terms are not synonymous, the issues involved in one are not necessarily the issues involved in the other. And they are right!

Certification issues revolve around the state's authorization to certify (license) professional personnel employed in the public schools. Teacher education questions involve problems about how to prepare a person to be qualified to obtain the certificate (license). It is almost impossible to deal with competency-based teacher education without also considering certification (hence the confusion, the overlapping) but certification issues can be considered in isolation from the problems of preparation. The focus in this chapter will be on the "certification" issues.

In most states an office of teacher education and certification exists and a relatively small group of professional personnel have the responsibility for issuing certificates and for developing new approaches to certification. The leadership in promoting competency-based certification emanates from these individuals.

Shared Assumptions

State certification officials, despite differences over the competency-based system each wants to establish, do share a number of basic assumptions:

Theodore E. Andrews is Director, Multi-State Consortium on Performance-Based Teacher Education, New York State Education Department.

Competency-based certification can be defined. While all interested states might define it differently, I would offer the following as basic to any definition: specific objective criteria are used as standards of measure.

Another assumption is that the present system for certifying teachers is either inadequate or could be vastly improved. The criticism here is more likely of the teacher education preparation than of the actual certifying system. Most states have worked out the details of processing certificates efficiently. They, however, have become more and more concerned that the persons receiving those certificates are not adequately prepared for the needs of the learner.

Unless one knows what a teacher is expected to do, to know, to feel (the definition of teaching), it is impossible to set up any kind of system. Persons who believe teaching is an art which defies definition reject this assumption.

It is assumed that objective systems of measuring performance are now available, or will be soon. Once one makes explicit the responsibilities of the teacher, it is possible to devise objective systems to decide whether or not the person possesses those desired behaviors. The explosion of interaction instruments now available for analyzing classroom behavior, the increasingly sophisticated use of behavioral objectives even in the affective area, and the rapidly spreading development of teacher education modules indicate that much is available and more is being produced daily.

An additional assumption is that enough is known about the relationship between teacher behavior and pupil learning to devise a certification system based on objective criteria. Most persons promoting this method of certifying teachers recognize that more research needs to be done. However, they realize that a system can be devised even now (without a broad research base) that relates program objectives to the candidates' performance. For example, sufficient research may not exist at present to indicate a direct relationship between the affective climate in a classroom and pupil learning. However, persons responsible for certification programs may have decided (based on the best professional judgment available and some conflicting research) that when teachers are supportive of student needs, students learn more. A certification policy can be based on measuring the performance level of those who wish to become teachers, using criteria, some of which are at best "guesstimates," of those who established the criteria. It is not based on the far stronger evidence that research has indicated that without exception all children learn more when teachers act in a supporting manner.

A final assumption is that educators should move *now* for the development of competency-based certification policies. They should wait no longer. Many people feel this is already a national movement and much of that leadership has come from certification officials.

Variety of State Plans

What system of competency-based teacher education should a state use? The approaches that the various states are taking to this are more different than alike and are for the most part in the developmental stage. The description of one policy today may be outdated even by the time of the publication of this book.

The American Association of Colleges for Teacher Education completed a national survey in September, 1971 which revealed that 32 states were at various stages of commitment to competency-based teacher education (from mild interest to initial implementation). Almost all of these states responded that they were anticipating moving through an approved program approach. (Persons completing approved programs receive certificates simply upon recommendation of the preparatory agency or agencies.) Moving through the approved program route makes those who are preparing teachers decide the most difficult questions (e.g., What performance criteria? How are they evaluated?). Certification officials in those states are developing new standards for program approval. Process standards describing how decisions must be made and by whom are the most common approach (e.g., Washington and New York). Florida, in addition to revising its regulations, is also providing leadership in developing the tools (performance modules, research, workshops) colleges and school districts will need.

Some few states are attempting to develop a state system to grant certification based on the candidates' demonstrated performance. In New Jersey, where qualified teams labored long to establish behavioral objectives for specific certification areas, the focus is now on finding the appropriate instruments and techniques for analyzing these behaviors. Arizona is developing a plan for recertification where the ultimate criterion will be pupil learning. The emphasis there is on product (pupil) objectives by using behavioral objectives clearly related to pupil learning.

Should the Educational System Change?

Are we only talking about changing the preparation of teachers through the certification system or are we really talking about changing the entire educational system? Some proponents feel that this is simply an attempt to "better" prepare teachers. Others believe competency-based certification policies will lead to the development of competency-based educational programs for pupils in public schools and that is really what is being attempted. And some feel that the development of competency-based certification policies based on explicit descriptions of the objectives and purposes of the schools will cause schools to change; hence the competency-based certification approach is really a vehicle for promoting change within the educational establishment.

Professional Involvement

Is the involvement of other professionals necessary? The basic question is whether a competency-based certification policy can be established and promoted in isolation from professional educators both in the public schools and in the colleges in a given state. Most people feel that competency-based education needs a broad base of support and that proponents must take the appropriate steps to provide involvement of representatives of teachers, collegiate personnel, lay citizens, boards of education, and students throughout the developmental stage so that whatever is established can be implemented.

Measurement Problems

Are the main issues "only measurement problems"? My assumption, from having visited many states and worked with a variety of educators in competency-based education, is that they divide into the two broad categories: the measurement people (the researchers who really were the foundation for this movement) and the humanists. It might be easier to constrast the difference in the two positions by characterizing the main priority of one group as "How do we measure performance?" and the main priority of the other group as "How do we bring about desirable change in the school system?" The people in the competency-based movement are concerned about both categories, seldom only one. However, their main emphasis is very often at one extreme of those two positions. The state directors of teacher education and certification who are promoting competency-based certification share this dichotomy and one can often tell the state viewpoint by analyzing the system they are promoting.

Promoting Competency-Based Certification

Given the interest of some thirty states and the work already done, it is possible to see some of the more evident problems that develop when promoting a competency-based certification system.

From Objective Data to
Subjective Decision

It is easy to analyze objectively a teacher's performance, using many of the presently available interaction instruments. However, it is relatively difficult to make a jump from the analysis of the data, which is objective, to a decision on whether or not that person should be issued a certificate. Another related problem is caused by the absolute necessity of the role of the certified person. There is great difficulty in establishing a competency-based certification system without first conceptualizing and defining in specific terms the role (or roles) of the professional person who will receive the certificate. This is a doubly difficult task because there is no clear consensus on this issue. For instance, should all teachers be able to ask open-ended questions (a favorite illustration because it can be measured objectively and it is relatively common to most teacher preparation programs)? The problems that spin out of that one issue would include:

(a) Do all teachers need to ask open-ended questions?
(b) Are some open-ended questions more desirable than others?
(c) How often should teachers ask open-ended questions?
(d) Is there any research that proves that teachers who ask open-ended questions achieve greater learning on the part of the pupils?

The problem isn't that these are unresolvable issues; the problem is that in order to establish a state system some consensus must be made on such basic issues. As long as states push those problems out to the preparation agencies (whether the colleges prepare teachers or whether a consortium of representative groups, as many states are now promoting, does it), those issues are not being resolved at the state level. The states, however, that are promoting their own competency-based certification programs must face those issues at the state level and must obtain some form of consensus on literally thousands of such issues before they can develop a program.

Lack of Research

The lack of research is a tremendous deterrent to the successful implementation at the present time of a competency-based certification policy. It is undoubtedly an improvement to develop a policy that describes the specific teaching skills of the candidate to be licensed. However, that is still a long way from guaranteeing that the teachers so licensed or so trained are going to be able to be effective teachers in the classroom—that children will learn. Many educators are concerned about the research implications and are devoting money and time to narrowing this gap; the gap must be narrowed and hopefully the effort is underway.

Politics of Local Educational Systems

Many states engaged in promoting competency-based certification are spending a considerable amount of that effort engaged in the politics of local education systems. The demands by the teaching profession for greater authority over the licensing of teachers, the militancy of teacher groups—both union and professional associations—the distrust that often exists between the practitioners in the field (e.g., the teachers) and those that in some sense control the teachers (e.g., the state education department) are long-founded and hard to diminish. As a result, state education agencies find they must spend an exorbitant amount of time in building trust before they can start to construct bridges. Agencies that refuse to do this may never achieve the consensus needed for the implementation of a competency-based program despite the quality of the program devised by the department personnel.

Inadequate Financial Support

Almost all states are suffering from a lack of funds, which has resulted in cutbacks in staff, a lack of funds to travel to out-of-state activities that may be absolutely necessary for planning to develop a competency-based certification program, and the inability to hire desperately needed consultants at the appropriate times. The USOE has helped, and several foundation awards to colleges indicate that funding agencies are concerned about the problem and are willing to fill some of this gap. Nonetheless, sufficient funds are not available; the movement is being promoted without an adequate financial base.

Changing Relationships

The relationships between colleges, teachers and state education departments also are undergoing change. Many departments are forcing consortium arrangements on people who are semireluctant or at best unskilled at such activities, and totally new relationships are developing.

Management System

A major problem facing state departments is developing a system to manage the formulation and implementation of competency-based certification. Because resources are usually allocated on a need basis, the requisite planning often has not taken place. The USOE has funded a nine-state consortium to help each of the participating states develop a management approach to the establishment of a competency-based teacher education and certification policy. The activities of this consortium should be helpful to all states. Whether a state is involved in the consortium or not, such planning must be done and the sooner it is done, the more likely the system will develop in appropriate directions.

Without doubt the 30 states considering competency-based education and certification will soon become 50. The problems and the solutions in one may well be helpful to others. The certification issues, however, may be the "glue" that will hold the movement together.

14

Accreditation and
Performance-Based Teacher Education

Lorraine R. Gay and
K. Fred Daniel

Accreditation has been defined as "the process whereby an organization or agency recognizes a college or university or a program of study as having met certain predetermined qualifications or standards" (Selden, 1960). Institutions desiring accreditation are generally evaluated initially and reviewed periodically to determine their compliance with the predetermined standards or criteria.

State accreditation is frequently confused with certification, which Kinney (1964) defines as "a process of legal sanction, authorizing the holder of a credential to perform specific services in the public schools of the state." Accreditation is granted to institutions, certification to individuals. State accreditation and certification are closely related, however, in that the state accredits teacher education programs primarily to control the quality of those to be certified for teaching (Mayor, 1965).

In the late nineteenth century the number and varieties of educational institutions were rapidly growing. In order to provide the controls needed to assure a standard of quality, accreditation—a process unique to the United States—was born. It is unique in that regulation of institutions by regional accrediting associations is voluntary. Non-governmental accrediting agencies are lacking in legal authority to compel institutions of higher learning

Lorraine R. Gay is Research Associate, Board of Regents, State University System of Florida, Tallahassee. K. Fred Daniel is Associate for Planning and Coordination, Department of Education, Tallahassee, Florida.

to become accredited. At least in theory, such institutions individually determine whether or not they will seek accreditation (Mayor, 1965). However, for many institutions the consequences of forgoing regional accreditation seem foreboding, thus making its pursuit essentially mandatory.

Accreditation has five major purposes: service to the public, institutional improvement, facilitating transfers, raising professional standards and information for prospective employers (Mayor, 1965). First, service to the public is performed by providing lists of accredited institutions or programs to persons in the process of selecting an institution either to attend or to be the recipient of grants. Second, institutional improvement is fostered through standards and criteria toward which they can strive and is further promoted by the self-study which is often required prior to the accreditation process. As some accrediting agencies emphasize improvement beyond minimum standards, positive change is often stimulated even in institutions of exceptional quality. Third, accreditation facilitates both intra- and inter-university transfer of students in that student records are evaluated in light of the accreditation status of the institution from which they come. Fourth, accreditation is a force in raising the educational standards of a profession. Almost every profession, including teaching, has adopted accreditation as a means of implementing its ideas concerning the preparation of practitioners. Finally, accreditation permits employers to evaluate more easily the quality of training of potential employees.

Accreditation in Teacher Education

Formal teacher training programs began in the nineteenth century as it came to be recognized that teachers required special training. Unlike all other professions, individuals were certified to teach before there were accredited teacher training programs.

Since its inception, accreditation in teacher education has been a controversial issue, especially with regard to national accreditation. This is attributable to a number of contributing factors which make accreditation in teacher education unique (Mayor, 1965). Programs in teacher education are offered by more institutions than any other professional field of study. As there is greater diversity of specialization within teacher education than in any other field of professional training, teacher education is dependent upon or related to more facets of a total institutional program than any other area of specialized accreditation. In addition, there are philosophical differences of opinion as to the optimal training procedures for teachers. There are some who question the classification of teaching as a profession and whether, if it is a profession, it is sufficiently homogeneous at all levels to justify a professional accrediting agency. Despite these problems, accreditation at the national, regional and state levels continues to be a strong force in the improvement of teacher training programs.

Types of Accreditation

National accreditation. The establishment of national accrediting processes was prompted as members of various professions sought to exercise greater control over the admission of additional members (Stinnett, 1969). Since regional associations generally concentrate on the general programs of an institution, the possibility of an institution with regional accreditation having one or more weak professional programs existed. In order to minimize tremendous variations in the quality of training programs, minimum standards and criteria were established by professional organizations. In teacher education the primary professional accrediting body is currently the National Council for the Accreditation of Teacher Education (NCATE). Contrary to general belief, NCATE does not differ greatly from other national professional organizations, in that none of the agencies has succeeded in basing accreditation on the quality of graduates. With respect to the need for flexibility of state requirements, it has been observed by Mayor (1965) that national accreditation, perhaps more than any other instrument, is in a position to contribute to the lessening of rigidity, and in fact, has already done so.

Regional accreditation. The first extralegal accrediting process to develop in the United States was the founding of the regional accrediting associations (Stinnett, 1969), which were needed because of the regional variations which existed in education. Despite marked diversities among regional associations, they all share in common four major purposes of accreditation (Selden, 1960). Initially, admissions and the maintenance of minimum academic standards were the two major concerns of regional accreditation. As more and more institutions have become accredited, however, increasing emphasis has been placed on the stimulation of educational self-improvement. The fourth major purpose of the regional accrediting is to serve, in Mayor's words, "as a countervailing force to the many external and internal pressures that are continually being exerted on our educational institutions."

State accreditation. Teacher certification has become almost exclusively the prerogative of state education agencies (SEAs), as they have increasingly assumed responsibility for teacher education (Daniel and Crenshaw, 1971). Basically, the SEAs' regulatory role in teacher education includes prescribing and administering minimum standards for the selection and training of educational personnel. Such standards have a major impact on the content of teacher education programs. Traditionally, standards for teacher education have consisted mainly of carefully prescribed course-credit requirements. A development of recent years is the approved program approach to teacher education and certification (Stinnett, 1969). The major purposes of this approach are to provide institutions with maximum autonomy in the development of teacher training programs and to reduce to a minimum state prescriptions for certification. Under the approved program approach, certification is granted primarily on the basis of graduation from an approved teacher training program. This approach permits each institution to develop training procedures which are consistent with its philosophy and resources, and which are responsive to local needs. The SEA, rather than prescribing specific courses and numbers of credits, simply determines the major areas which a program must include, e.g., educational psychology.

While the trend is for SEAs to adopt a program approval approach, agreement on the best basis for program approval has not yet been reached; most SEAs are anticipating further changes in standards or criteria within the next few years (Daniel and Crenshaw, 1971).

Relationships between national, regional and state accreditation. There are approximately 1,200 teacher training institutions in the United States, all of which are approved by their respective SEAs, with close to ninety percent of them also accredited by their respective regional associations (Stinnett, 1969). While fewer than forty percent of the training institutions are accredited by NCATE, those that are prepare approximately seventy-five percent of the new teachers each year. There is common agreement that there is need for even greater cooperation between national, regional and state accrediting agencies. The need for such cooperation is evident from the fact that all three types of accreditation affect at least six aspects of teacher education programs: structure and administration, curriculum, faculty policies, student policies, finances and experimentation and research (Mayor, 1965). In addition, such cooperation would reduce the time and effort required by an institution prior to, and during, accreditation visits.

**Current Status of
Performance-Based Accreditation**
Because of the nature of their relationship, changes in accreditation standards must necessarily follow changes in certification standards; if certification is based on carefully prescribed course-credit requirements, then programs seeking accreditation must verify that they provide such courses to preservice teachers. Similarly, if certification criteria are performance-based, teacher training programs must include stated competencies, instructional strategies for achieving these competencies and appropriate criterion-referenced evaluation techniques. A survey of state directors of teacher education has found that seven states are currently using a course-credit approach to certification, forty-two states are using an approved program approach, and one state is using a performance-based approach (Frinks, 1971). Further, six of the states currently using a course-credit approach expect to

change to an approved program approach—three within the next year or two. Twenty-three states currently using an approved program approach anticipate moving toward performance-based criteria—twelve within one or two years. Florida, New York, Washington, Texas and Minnesota are five major states which are working toward the implementation of performance-based teacher education. Being representative of varied approaches to implementation, the efforts of Florida, New York and Washington are herein briefly described.

Florida. In Florida, teaching certificates are awarded under both a course-credit approach and an approved program approach. The approved program approach is favored; eventually, it is planned that the program approval approach will be used exclusively and that performance-based programs will predominate.

To guide new teacher education efforts, three types of action have been taken (Daniel and Crenshaw, 1971). The first, by the State Teacher Education Advisory Council, was to begin developing guidelines for teacher education programs. The guidelines, intended to replace prescriptive standards for designing and evaluating teacher education programs, were expected to meet the following criteria: (1) they must cite behaviors of children to be affected by program graduates, (2) they must describe the corresponding competencies required by teachers, (3) they must describe the instructional strategies required for achievement of these competencies, (4) they must present candidate selection criteria and (5) they must include a plan for graduate follow-up relative to effectiveness. A second action taken by the Florida Department of Education was to advocate performance-based or competency-based curricula in teacher education. Third, in 1970, the SEA began seeking a new set of program approval standards to encourage institutions to develop alternative approaches to teacher education. The new standards require that all relevant sources of information be used in determining competencies to be included in a program and techniques of evaluation. The proposed new standards require that: (1) decision-making responsibility be clearly defined, (2) admission criteria be clearly defined, (3) procedures for determining when competency criteria have been met are specified, (4) procedures for dealing with individuals who do not meet performance criteria are specified, (5) procedures for designating persons who have completed the program are specified and (6) procedures for following up persons who have completed the program are specified. Thus, Florida's approach includes the development of guidelines for program development and the development of new program approval standards which encourage, rather than merely permit, the development of performance-based teacher education programs.

New York. The SEA of New York has established procedures for approval of teacher education programs which are closely related to certification policies (Daniel and Crenshaw, 1971). On-site program reviews are conducted by the SEA to assure that program graduates meet certification standards. Graduates of approved programs need not undergo a detailed transcript analysis in order to receive a teaching certificate. In 1968, New York certification standards were revised with specificity of requirements drastically reduced. The change in certification standards naturally carried with it a change in program approval standards. Thus, the removal of detailed requirements from certification standards was also a removal of detailed requirements from program approval standards.

In 1971, New York adopted a new set of "process standards" for teacher education program approval intended to promote the implementation of performance-based teacher education. The standards specify the processes which will be followed in implementing teacher education programs, and not the content. These process standards include four major elements: (1) the program must be planned, developed, monitored and evaluated by cooperating agencies acting as a policy board; (2) the program developers must address the questions "What are the student objectives and priorities of the schools involved?" and "What competencies should a teacher educator have to serve in those schools?"; (3) the program developers must specify procedures for measuring the mastery of competencies and the evidence which will be accepted; and (4) a management system must be established to provide continuous data for operating and evaluating the program. The nature of these standards indicates that in many ways New York is following the approaches of Washington.

Washington. The standards for teacher education program approval which have been used in Washington since 1961 are characterized by flexibility and are in the form of guidelines rather than detailed requirements (Daniel and Crenshaw, 1971). Having completed a four-year developmental effort, Washington has recently adopted a new set of standards for the approval of programs aimed at implementing performance-based teacher education. The standards are similar to New York's new process standards in that they specify the process of program development rather than the content. The criteria for approval include the following: (1) the program is based upon an analysis and description of the competency expectations for the particular professional role for which the program is designed; (2) the program is individualized, that is, individual needs and talents are cared for and learning tasks are chosen or assigned as a consequence of an individual's readiness to perform; (3) the program provides frequent and periodic feedback to participants concerning their performance; and (4) the program is offered by an agency which provides frequent and periodic performance feedback to their own faculty.

An important aspect of the standards is the stipulation for joint participation by school districts, universities and professional organizations in program development and implementation. The Washington standards also stipulate that a program should include competencies in subject matter specialties, pedagogy and personal characteristics. They depict the professional educator as a decision maker and include the ideas that professional preparation should continue throughout the career of the practitioner and that school organizations and professional associations should also be recognized as preparation agencies.

All three states have endorsed a performance-based approach to teacher education and are using a form of process standards. All are relying on local institutions to develop and implement programs, rather than specifying competencies from the state level.

"Competency-Based" and
"Non-Competency-Based" Accreditation

Since the initiation of state accreditation of teacher education programs, the question of standards has been a recurrent issue. Should the state seek to assure that the programs have desirable prerequisite conditions or inputs? Should the state seek to assure that the training processes have certain desirable characteristics or should the state focus on the competencies which teachers are expected to possess and not be concerned about the manner in which the competencies are developed (Daniel and Crenshaw, 1971)? The "tidal" shifts which have occurred in accreditation standards have reflected corresponding philosophical shifts concerning the proper regulatory role of the state.

Trends in Standards

There are essentially three types of standards which have been used in the evaluation of teacher education programs: input standards, process standards and product standards. Input standards specify quantitative criteria, such as number of Ph.D.s on the staff, number of books in the library and the number of square feet per student; process standards specify actions of the staff in implementing the planned program; product standards specify learning outcomes resulting from the implementation of a planned program. For many years accreditation was based primarily on input standards; there is increasing consensus that the only defensible basis for program evaluation is in terms of the competencies possessed by its graduates.

Since the beginning of certification in the nineteenth century, standards have undergone cyclic shifts; beginning with product criteria (use of examinations in elementary fields), the trend in standards has progressed through a product-process-input-process-product cycle coming full circle with the current advocacy of product criteria (competency-based teacher education movement). The search has been for standards which would assure effective public school teachers. Three types of standards—results from formal examinations, records of academic work and analysis of institutional characteristics—have been tried with varying degrees of success. Examinations were abandoned because the technology for measuring significant teacher competencies was not available; transcript analysis lost favor because the same words or symbols on different transcripts represent different levels of excellence; analysis of institutional characteristics has been questioned because the relationship between institutional traits and traits of graduates is uncertain. As will be discussed later, the current product standard movement is not free from many of the same problems which beset the original movement and led to its abandonment.

Competency-Based Accreditation

Nearly half of the states are currently planning to work toward performance-based criteria for teacher education. As illustrated by the discussion of the approaches of Florida, New York and Washington, the implementation strategies of the states are varied and yet similar. Correspondingly, there will be many commonalities, as well as disparities, between the accreditation standards of the states.

In formulating accreditation standards and related guidelines for program developers, the SEAs are faced with the task of determining what elements are essential and what elements are desirable in a performance-based teacher education program. In a 1971 publication of the American Association of Colleges for Teacher Education (AACTE), Elam presented the findings of the AACTE Committee on Performance-Based Teacher Education. Following a fifteen-month study, the committee concluded that there appears to be general agreement that a teacher education program is performance-based if:

1. *Competencies* (knowledge, skills, behaviors) to be demonstrated by program graduates are derived from explicit conceptions of teacher roles, stated in measurable terms and made public in advance;

2. *Criteria for assessing competencies* are congruent with specified competencies, make explicit expected levels of mastery under specified conditions and are made public in advance;

3. *Assessment of the student's competence* is based on his performance, takes into account evidence of his knowledge relevant to planning for, analyzing, interpreting or evaluating situations or behavior and strives for objectivity;

4. *The student's rate of progress through the program* is determined by demonstrated competence rather than by time or course completion; and

5. *The instructional program* is intended to facilitate the development and evaluation of the student's achievements of specified competencies.

The above listed factors are considered to be generic; the Committee has also compiled a list of elements classified as either implied or as related and desirable for a performance-based program. Foremost among them is the provision that instruction is individualized and personalized. As time, credits and courses are irrelevant dimensions in a performance-based program, and since students may enter with a variety of backgrounds, individualization is extremely desirable if not nearly essential. A second important element is the provision of adequate feedback, related to achievement of competencies, which serves as an indicator to the trainee and guides his progress through the program. Other desirable characteristics include a systematic program and design flexibility.

Systematic Program. Implementation of a product-oriented systems approach is normally a correlate of a performance-based approach to teacher education. The following are characteristics of a systematic program in performance-based teacher education: emphasis on exit, not entrance, requirements; modularized instruction; student accountability in terms of performance; field-centered instructional strategies; broad-based decision-making; and instruction which includes skill development and concept identification and utilization.

Design Flexibility. A characteristic of design flexibility is the provision that both the teachers and the students are designers of an instructional system which includes alternative instructional strategies for achievement of competencies. Another aspect of flexibility is the inclusion of a research component—the system is open and regenerative. A third element is that training is viewed as life-long rather than only preservice in nature. A fourth desirable factor is that role integration takes place as the trainee gains an increasingly comprehensive perception of teaching problems. The product-oriented nature of a performance-based teacher education program highlights the importance of feedback to the program from trainees and graduates, but more importantly, from employers of graduates. Such feedback is the basis of continual program revision designed to increase the meaningfulness and relevance of training.

Issues and Problems

The question of standards for accreditation of teacher education programs has always been a serious problem for SEAs. Further, in addition to problems which are common to accreditation in all professional fields (e.g., accreditation procedures), there are a number of special problems generally associated with teacher education (Mayor, 1965). These include: the problem of giving status to professional courses, the problem of overlapping jurisdiction in accreditation, the problem of restricting the national accrediting agency's jurisdiction over certain aspects of professional programs and the problem of accrediting specialized areas in the profession.

Accreditation of performance-based programs, a relatively new phenomenon, entails a number of new issues. A major concern is the issue of how or by whom the competencies expected of trainees should be derived. Until such time as teacher competencies are empirically identified as being related to pupil learning, SEAs will have no irrefutable basis on which to require the inclusion of specific competencies in a teacher education program. Hence, it is likely that program developers will enjoy a great deal of freedom in selecting those competencies which are most suitable to their overall goals. While a real danger exists that only those competencies will be chosen which are easy to describe and evaluate, evaluation of selection can only be done on the basis of the selection procedures followed. The problem of what constitutes sufficient input for effective decision-making is as yet unresolved.

Another major issue involves evaluation of a program's effectiveness: where does the program's responsibility end? Does it end when the trainee has successfully achieved all specified competencies and has been awarded a certificate? Is the institution also accountable for on-the-job performance? Turner (1971) has presented six levels of criteria at which trainees can be evaluated. Under criterion level six, information is collected on the teacher's understanding of behavior, concepts or principles; under criterion level one, information is collected on the behavior of the teacher in the classroom and also on the pupil outcomes which are associated with that performance. Turner believes that teacher education programs should be responsible only through criterion level three, whereby information is collected on the performance of the teacher in the classroom. He believes that performance over time should affect extended certification but should not reflect on the quality of the training institution. As discussed earlier, feedback from employers is an important element in program revision. Whether this feedback should be considered in the accreditation process has not yet been determined, although there is agreement that a plan for receiving such feedback should be required.

A major problem in a performance-based program is that of management. It is likely that any given "course" includes a number of teacher competencies. Thus the record keeping task alone is considerably magnified, as data must be kept on achievement of competencies rather than on courses completed or credits earned. Another management concern is the problem of transfer students from non-performance-based programs. A traditional transcript would not provide adequate information for placement in a performance-based program. As graduation from an approved program is often the prime prerequisite for certification, accreditation standards must include a provision for the existence of an adequate management system.

Accreditation standards have come full circle with the current trend toward product standards brought about by the performance-based teacher education movement. The technology necessary for successful implementation is largely available. Further progress would appear to depend more on consensus regarding desirability and on the existence of a spirit of cooperation in working toward the solution of the major problems than on the development of new techniques.

References

Daniel, K.F. and J.W. Crenshaw. *What Has Been and Should Be the Role of State Education Agencies in the Development and Implementation of Teacher Education Programs (Both Pre- and Inservice)? A Review and Analysis of Literature.* Prepared for the Bureau of Educational Personnel Development, Division of Assessment and Coordination, United States Office of Education, Order No. OEC-0-71-3315, September 1971.

Elam, S. Performance-Based Teacher Education: What Is the State of the Art? *Bulletin of the American Association of Colleges for Teacher Education,* 1971, *24* (9).

Frinks, M.L. An Analytical Study of Teacher Certification Processes as Perceived by Leadership Personnel Within the Teacher Education and Certification Sections of the Fifty State Education Agencies with Special Emphasis on the Development of the Performance-Based Movement. Unpublished doctoral dissertation, University of Massachusetts, 1971.

Kinney, L.B. *Certification in Education.* Englewood Cliffs, New Jersey: Prentice-Hall, 1964.

Mayor, J.R. *Accreditation in Teacher Education: Its Influence on Higher Education.* Washington, D.C.: National Commission on Accrediting, 1965.

Selden, W.K. *Accreditation: A Struggle over Standards in Higher Education.* New York: Harper and Brothers, 1960.

Stinnett, T.M. Teacher Education, Certification and Accreditation. In E. Fuller and J.B. Pearson (Eds.) *Education in the States: National Development Since 1900.* Washington, D.C.: National Education Association of the United States, 1969, Chapter 9.

Turner, R.L. Levels of Criteria. In B. Rosner (Ed.) *The Power of Competency-Based Teacher Education: Final Report of the Committee on National Program Priorities in Teacher Education.* Washington, D.C.: National Center for Educational Research and Development, Office of Education, United States Department of Health, Education, and Welfare, July 1971.

The authors wish to express their appreciation to Charles B. Reed for his helpful comments and suggestions regarding the content of this article.

15

Relating Communications Technology to Competency-Based Education

Charles C. Wall and
Richard C. Williams

Introduction

The purpose of this chapter is to examine possible relationships between recent developments in communication technology and Competency-Based Education (CBE). The chapter is divided into two parts: In Part I we speculate on how two basic education features that have typically been the province of schools can be provided by alternate means. These alternatives may well revolutionize the purposes and structure of schooling as we now know it. In Part II we discuss some conditions and resulting knotty problems that must be faced if any technology-based evolution of our schooling system is to become a reality.

I. Into the Future

As never before, we have some real alternatives to consider in designing a schooling system. This makes planning both exciting and exceedingly difficult. People are hesitant, for a variety of reasons, to abandon that with which they are familiar. Also, it is difficult to undergo the critical task of maintaining the existing system while at the same time designing and implementing the new. Assuming that such a dilemma can be managed, what might the educational system of the future be like and how will CBE contribute to the new design?

Charles C. Wall is Coordinator of Product Development, Research Division, I/D/E/A, Los Angeles, California. **Richard C. Williams** is Assistant Dean, Graduate School of Education, University of California at Los Angeles.

By the turn of the century (2000 A.D.), we speculate that schools will have undergone a fundamental change. Advanced communications technology, coupled with CBE, will provide two of the basic features traditionally provided by schools: (1) providing information and training, and (2) certifying the quality of student performance. It will generally become more convenient and economical to provide these features outside of what we have known as a traditional school building.

Information and training, heretofore provided by teachers and pupils in a classroom, will be offered by a vast array of communications devices that will make it possible for the learner to receive instruction in a variety of settings, and the learner can pick out that which is most important for him. A variety of tools will break our dependence on the typical classroom teaching setting. Some such devices are: audio and video cassettes that can be played through a television receiver, and miniature computer terminals in each home attached by satellites to information banks throughout the world that will expand the speed and accuracy of learning. Holography, a concept that just a few years ago was thought to be wild speculation but today is a reality, will allow free-standing three-dimensional images to outdate the television set. Three-dimensional films are already in the laboratory production stage of development.

Through technology, students will have access to the best teachers and the most carefully thought out and executed learning experiences. The numerous traditional school buildings that are found in cities today will be replaced by a few Community Learning Centers, conveniently located for all to use.

Most important, learning will be a lifetime activity not restricted by age or subject matter. Except as noted later in this chapter, people will learn what they want, when they want and at their own speed.

The certifying role of the schools will be met, in part, by the use of CBE techniques. In many types of learning activities, CBE can be used to certify that the learner has achieved a given level of proficiency at some point in his learning experience. This technique is useful in determining whether the learner can perform a given task, e.g., repair a typewriter, keep a set of books, or whether he has mastered a given skill so that he can move on to more advanced learning, e.g., addition, subtraction and multiplication, prior to studying division. At the completion of instruction, the learner could either be tested via computer in his home, or he could visit a community evaluation center where a CBE examination could be administered and his proficiency could be certified. CBE cannot be used to assess proficiency in those fields of study where clear criteria of performance cannot be identified. However, as work continues in the development of CBE, we assume that some techniques will be developed for those learning activities for which CBE activities presently seem to have limited application. Thus, through the linking of advanced communications technology with CBE, the need for two essential functions now performed by the schools will be provided through other means.

For purposes of illustration, it might be useful to give an example of how this application of communications technology and CBE might work. Let us suppose that a learner wants to become an accountant. Initially our accountant trainee could be given a test, through his home computer terminal or at the Community Learning Center, to determine whether he has the prerequisite mathematical and conceptual skills. Assuming the pretest results show that he has these skills, he would then subscribe to a program that would utilize one or more of several media techniques (e.g., cable television, audio-visual cassettes) that would provide a carefully sequenced package of instruction. Upon the completion of parts or all of the instructional program, he could sit for a criterion-referenced examination. Upon successful completion of all examinations, he would be certified as having attained a given level of proficiency. This achievement may enable him to enter into either some supervised field work under the aegis of an experienced accountant, or as a beginning accountant.

Not all of the accountant's training would be completed in the home. His field supervision would have to be provided by some schooling agency, likewise some of his materials might have to be provided in some central location (Community Learning Center). In addition, it may be necessary for the Community

Learning Center to provide human tutorial help for those who feel they could profit from such assistance.

Schools as we know them will change considerably in their appearance, role and function. Much of the instruction-giving process will be provided by the use of advanced communications media, while CBE will satisfy the certifying function. Three essential elements will still need to be provided: (1) There are some activities that simply are not possible to learn entirely in the home or the small group learning centers. One thinks of chemistry or physics, which require extensive laboratory equipment. These activities are reserved for the Community Learning Center which will house a wide variety of equipment, laboratories and other facilities. (2) There is the need to provide for the social and personal dimensions of man. One thinks of such activities as counseling and discussions of important personal, ethical and aesthetic topics with other human beings. There are severe limits on the uniquely human needs that can be accommodated by machines. Commmunity Learning Centers will increasingly take on the satisfying of human needs. Such institutions would be manned by persons skilled in helping people solve personal problems and realize their human potential, e.g., psychologists, family and guidance counselors, sociologists and interesting and resourceful human beings who can provide encouragement and excitement to the lives of fellow humans. (3) Certain occupations will require that the learner engage in practice in the field under the guidance of a skilled practitioner.

Readily Available Education

In summary, we envision a society in which education for occupational competency or for more effective use of leisure time will be more readily available to all through the use of advanced communications technology. What is more, it will be available more at the learner's convenience, and he can achieve a given level of competency at his own rate of speed. It really doesn't matter that one learner takes half again as long to master some skill as someone else. What is important is that he gain a given level of competency and, through techniques that come under the rubric of Competency-Based Education, he will be able to certify to himself and others that he has achieved at a given level of proficiency.

Once these techniques are developed and more readily available, educators can concentrate on those unique human functions that can be accomplished only through human inter-action in small or large groups. Community Learning Centers will be manned by those who possess those skills and talents that are valued and demanded by society and can be provided only by fellow humans.

II. Problems to Face

The future we have projected is not predestined. It can be achieved only through intelligent planning. If we are to realize the events described in this chapter, there are several problems that must be solved. Three of these problems are: (1) the production of hardware, (2) the development of software and (3) political and economic constraints.

The Production of Hardware

In a very real sense hardware appears to be the least serious problem. Many technological advances have been made that have implications for a new educational system, such as cable television, combined sound and video cassettes, compact terminals for homes, holography, transmission of images through laser beams, and computers giving movement and voice to a single piece of art work.

A serious problem confronting technological hardware is not the lack of ideas and practical innovation, but the extremely high cost of research, development and dissemination. Many hardware manufacturers cannot sell their present products. This high cost of production results in a self-defeating cycle of events. If current products cannot be sold in large quantities, there is little inducement on the part of the manufacturers to devote greater amounts of scarce resources to developing new generations of hardware. As a result, the cost to the consumer is so high that few advanced technological systems are being purchased and used by educators. Only when the demand for such products rises and the costs drop, because of the economics of mass production, will this cycle be broken. We speculate that the increasing cost of labor (teachers) will eventually motivate the public to seek alternative schooling methods, and the economics and utility of a more technology-based system will be apparent.

Another problem is the great lack of standardization of similar products among manufacturers. Each manufacturer is attempting to produce a piece of equipment that is just a little different and hopefully a little better than the others in his field. A wide variety of incompatible products has resulted in making those who purchase such equipment in education leery of their usefulness. No purchasing agent wants to be so restricted by a piece of hardware that he must buy supplies and replacements from one source because all other equipment and materials are incompatible. It appears, however, that in some product lines the compatibility problem is being attacked where demand is sufficiently high, e.g., videotape equipment.

The Development of Technical Software

There is a tremendous "software lag" in developing and implementing a technology for a CBE system. Only recently has television, for example with *Sesame Street,* begun to have any apparently consistent, planned impact on the education of American children. This is not to say television has not influenced our society. *Sesame Street* is an example of how we have begun to design programs with a pedagogical purpose.

There are two important reasons for this "software lag." One is the vast disparity between the amount of money that has been invested in hardware versus that spent on software. The entire space program, for example, has had an enormous impact on the development of transistors and other components that make up the technical systems. Public support of software development has been quite limited and sporadic. No real advances will be made until vast development money, public and private, is made available on an as yet unprecedented scale.

Another hindrance is that we are overly constrained by our

traditional assumptions about teaching and learning. We are a "schooled society" and as such, schools have an inordinate influence on our thinking about education. As a result, we tend to think of learning taking place when a teacher is present with a class of 20-30 pupils. Similarly, our training of teachers has centered largely around the management of such teaching situations. These teaching settings place heavy constraints on the use of truly individualized instructional techniques. It is not surprising that teachers seldom think about utilizing sophisticated teaching techniques when they are heavily burdened with the pressing environment of a roomful of pupils. Thus, teachers are not trained in utilizing new technological tools nor are they given an environment in which the utilization of such tools is realistic. As a result, they do not demand such techniques and it is not profitable for manufacturers to invest heavily in software development.

The application of CBE is but another example of this dilemma. Many are aware of the usefulness of this instructional system. Yet, while its value is acknowledged, it is doubtful that it will gain widespread use until teachers are freed from the constraints of the typical classroom.

Political Problems

We anticipate that a very formidable challenge to the expanded use of communications technology and CBE will result when these techniques clash with the economic interests of established occupations and professions.

Most occupations and professions limit the supply of practitioners so that there will not be a "flooding of the market" with qualified people who will drive down the cost of services by competing vigorously for jobs. This supply has been limited in part by controlling the number and kinds of people who can receive authorized training either in trade or professional schools or through apprentice programs. Thus, many people who have the basic aptitude to become practitioners are denied the opportunity to enter the field because they cannot afford the training, or because there are not enough openings in the schools or apprentice programs that provide the training. This control of the supply of practitioners is important to these occupations as it has a direct effect on their economic well-being.

Technology, coupled with CBE, will provide a means whereby individuals with an interest in and aptitude for specialized training can receive basic instruction on their own, independent of the control of the professions or skilled trades. Through criterion tests they can demonstrate their proficiency in what they have learned.

It is reasonable to expect that when practitioners in these occupations see the potential of these technical tools to wrest from them the control over the supply of qualified practitioners, they will seek political means to protect their economic interests. This will provide a serious test of the degree to which communications technology and CBE will be used to provide occupational training on a vast scale. Because of such pressures, we anticipate that the application of advanced communications technology and CBE will be developed in those fields where the economic interests of a segment of the population are not threatened.

16

The Human Side of
Competency-Based Education

Alfred S. Alschuler
and Allen Ivey

Holding students accountable for mastery of irrelevant knowledge
defeats them and the purposes of humane education. Obviously,
the first task in establishing competency-based education is to
determine what is relevant both to students and to society. There
are extensive data suggesting that if teachers were completely
faithful to the needs of students in preparing them for an
effective, satisfying life after school, there would be a dramatic
shift in emphasis from academic curricula to psychological and
vocational curricula.

This prospect raises important ethical issues which need to be
considered in detail. Especially important is the issue of imposing
values, always a difficult problem, but even more complex when
dealing with psychological education. The existential concept of
intentionality, when operationally defined, offers one way of
freeing, rather than limiting, students' value choices. In the
remainder of this chapter we will discuss these issues in greater
detail in hopes that advocates of competency-based education will
not allow mortis to accompany their new educational rigor.

What Is Important to Learn?

Most of what is taught in schools (as measured by grades) is
unrelated to career advancement, citizenship or psycho-socially
healthy adulthood. In three separate reviews of the empirical
research, virtually no strong correlations existed between grades

Alfred S. Alschuler and **Allen Ivey** are at the University of Masschusetts.

130

and success in non-technical jobs, teaching, engineering, medicine, or to social status, citizenship activities and cultural interests (Hoyt, 1965; Kirschenbaum, Simon and Napier, 1971) or to adult mental health, after intelligence and social class are partialled out (Kohlberg, La Cross and Ricks, 1970). This has been the stark but consistent conclusion in over thirty years of research. The absence of strong relationships between grades and life success is due partially to the fact that grading is so unreliable that it is invalid. Stripped of its bogus objectivity, "marking" students is a degrading event for the human beings involved. Good teachers know this intuitively but are victims of a hierarchical system of requirements based on grades. Even when competence in academic subject matter *is* measured reliably through standardized tests, the relationship to life success is weak. In contrast, how long people stay in school, as distinct from what they learn, *is* related to several indices of life success. However, this correlation is due primarily to job entrance requirements based purely on number of years of schooling, rather than on the practical value of what was learned during those additional years. Both life success and the number of years of schooling are consequences of good intelligence and social class background. The correlation between length of schooling and life success thereby reflects their common causes rather than being indicative of valuable learning in school. Several recent Supreme Court decisions reflect this conclusion by demanding proof from employers that their prerequisites for jobs have established relationships to job success.

If students are held accountable for mastery of irrelevant knowledge, they have a number of unfortunate alternatives. When students sense a discrepancy between what teachers require and what life demands, it undermines their trust in the wisdom of their teachers. In such a situation they can hypocritically let themselves be coerced or they can choose to be punished for refusing to accept irrelevant learning tasks. Neither choice increases the dignity of their presence in school. If, on the other hand, students believe in the value of what is being taught, when in fact it is not important, then students develop an inaccurate view of reality, and schooling is systematically misleading. Logically it is obvious that in such a case, less of this harmful schooling would be better, in contrast to international rhetoric proclaiming universal public education as an inalienable Right and Good. There is some supporting evidence for this anti-establishment point of view. Elkind (1969) summarized a number of empirical studies by proposing that "the longer we delay formal instruction, up to certain limits, the greater the period of plasticity and the higher the level of achievement." In a similar vein, Husen (1967), in his study of achievement in mathematics in 12 countries, concluded that the more years students were enrolled in school prior to testing at the age of 12, the more *negative* their attitude toward school. We are not suggesting that competency-based education be abolished, but only that educators be held accountable for creating instructional objectives that define relevant human competence. Otherwise, the "effectiveness" of competency-based education means effectively coercing students, effectively exposing teachers' incorrect view of reality, effectively misleading children about what is necessary to survive and flourish in society.

There are two areas important to life success that are not receiving sufficient attention in education. While the majority of human, physical and financial resources are spent on teaching academic curricula, the majority of students need vocational and psychological curricula. Of the approximately fifty million students, about forty million will not complete college. Fifteen million will not even complete high school. This staggering number of drop-outs will enter the labor market by-and-large unprepared because only six million will have had any significant amount of vocational training. Teaching important psychological processes is equally ignored and absent in spite of massive evidence showing its relationship to life success. The nationwide Coleman report (1966) indicated that a student's psychological attitude toward his destiny (whether it was controlled more by himself or by fate) and his self-concept were more strongly related to how much students learned than all other factors combined—teacher preparation, physical facilities, textbooks, etc. Yet there are no widely used curricula to teach either fate-control or positive self-concept. Similarly, in their thorough review of the research on childhood predictors of adult mental health, Kohlberg, La Cross and Ricks (1970) found that the two best predictors of all forms of adult maladjustment (e.g., psychoses, alcoholism, criminal acts) were poor peer relationships during the first three years of schooling and anti-social behavior during the second three years of schooling. Kohlberg *et al.* argue that these behaviors reflect immaturity in cognitive and ego development because, conversely, relatively high levels of cognitive and ego development during these periods seem to inoculate students permanently against later forms of severe adult maladjustment. Nevertheless, there are no psychological curricula in schools to promote cognitive and ego development even though relevant psychological education courses have been developed. This is an understandable, but not excusable, time lag in the dissemination of innovations. The conservative nature of schooling (perhaps "preservative" is more accurate) mitigates against quick adoption. However, it would be neither understandable nor excusable if educational innovators merely rewrote the existing educational objectives as cast-iron competency criteria. This would make competency-based education into a truly preservative solution for embalming the status quo. However, to seize the opportunity created by the national interest in competency-based education to introduce relevant psychological objectives raises immediate ethical issues, which require discussion.

Ethical Issues in Psychological Education

Competency-based psychological education raises clear, direct concerns about psychological imperialism, coercion not of the data students interpret, but of the far more basic process of interpreting the data they get. Ultimately, holding children accountable for their psychological development requires philosophic, religious and political decisions about the desirable nature of human goodness. Without attempting to resolve such a debate through this chapter, it is possible, nevertheless, to indicate the most salient concerns raised by psychological education.

Although schools have the responsibility for preparing effective citizens for society, parents balk when teachers interpret their mandate to include attitudes, motives and values. Increasingly, adolescents are objecting just as strenuously to psychological goals chosen by both parents and teachers. Even more than the content of the choice, students want to keep for themselves the process of choosing. Yet, a student tyranny over the content and processes of psychological education is an abdication of legitimate responsibility by adults who must live with the social consequences of student choices; for instance, what would happen to the human beings in the student's life if he did not learn basic skills in decision-making and in decent human relations? Ideally there should be reciprocity and equality among those involved in the choice of psychological goals.

These considerations of how goals are to be chosen ignore the equally important question of content. What are the goals of psychological education? In a recent review of the existing psychological education courses, Alschuler (1973) identified four clusters of goals with associated rationales legitimizing them: (1) to promote the humane psycho-social aims of education; (2) to teach processes that are useful to students in reaching the goals they choose; (3) to increase positive mental health; and (4) to foster normative development. Each of these desirable end states responds to practical ethical questions such as: good for what? good for whom? good for when? These answers make informed, intentional choices possible. For instance, in response to these "what," "who" and "when" questions we can state that Achievement Motivation Training helps mid- to upper-level business (McClelland and Winter, 1969) and adolescents (Alschuler, Tabor and McIntyre, 1970) become more effective in their pursuit of excellence in work, hobbies and sports. The course itself concentrates on teaching the pattern of achievement planning and on consulting with students to determine if they have a specific achievement goal for which this action strategy would be useful. This collaborative process enhances students' ability to reach the goals they choose. In extensive evaluation studies of achievement motivation programs for adolescents (Alschuler, 1973), approximately one-third of the students had made "major" applications of the course one-and-a-half years later. But note—the measure of course effectiveness is not some preordained inventory of specific behaviors, but instead a reliably coded rating of the extent and detail of the students' voluntary application. This criterion of competency allows teachers to set performance objectives for themselves (e.g., 33 percent making "major" voluntary applications one year after the course) without forcing any individual student to do any specific achievement activity. The essential characteristic of this system that avoids the thornier ethical issues is to encourage students to make their own choices within a broad but well-defined class of behaviors of known relevance. This characteristic deserves further clarification.

Intentionality:
A Metagoal of Psychological Education
 Intentionality is the process of fusing conscious consideration of alternatives with positive action. Individuals who act intentionally can generate alternative behaviors in a given situation and can come at a problem from different points of view as they receive environmental feedback. Equally important, individuals who act intentionally are not bound to one course of action, but can respond effectively to an ever-changing environment (Ivey, 1969). Intentionality is a general competency in which individuals have numerous alternatives for achieving their particular ends. Thus, intentionality is simultaneously a metagoal and a process for attaining specific objectives. It frees rather than coerces individuals.

 Several illustrations may be helpful in understanding how intentionality is related to life success. The psychological competencies of the intentional individual have been defined for a curriculum in human relations. Specific modules within this curriculum include "relaxation," "non-verbal communication," "listening," "self-expression," "decision-making," "behavior change through dynamic and existential psychology" and "combatting personal and institutional racism." Each competency module is presented to students as an alternative for psychological growth. When students have all of these competencies in their repertoires, they have alternatives available when one or more is unsuccessful in solving a problem and a greater chance to determine their own destinies. Training techniques that facilitate attainment of these behavioral objectives have been tested in a variety of educational settings from elementary schools to mental hospitals (Ivey, 1972; Ivey and Rollin, 1971).

A more detailed presentation of one competency, listening, indicates the potential of competency-based psychological education for building intentionality. Attending behavior was originally developed as a counselor/therapist training skill within micro-counseling, a video tape-feedback method of counselor training (Ivey, 1972). Operationally defined, listening consists of three specific observable behaviors: (1) eye contact, (2) physical attention and (3) verbal following. Data from counselor and therapist research revealed that this skill cluster was teachable and important in counselor and client interaction (Ivey *et al.,* 1968). Moreland (1971) found that therapists who could consciously control their listening processes were better prepared to help others in a variety of interviewing situations. In subsequent work, Rollin (1970) demonstrated that teachers can learn to become more effective listeners. Aldridge (1971) has extended the training to junior high pupils on the assumption that developing effective listening skills can facilitate more learning and better peer relationships. Being able to listen provides students with the ability to communicate more fully with others. This skill creates more, rather than fewer, alternatives.

Students' Moral Reasoning

In another application of intentionality, Blatt and Kohlberg (1970) are developing educational procedures for increasing the level of students' moral reasoning. This is not surprising, given Kohlberg's finding (cited earlier) that moral development in pre-adolescents is strongly related to the absence of adult mental illness. Kohlberg's six operationally defined levels of moral reasoning reflect a decrease in egocentrism and an increase in the number of alternative points of view that can be kept in mind while making moral decisions. Therefore, higher level moral reasoning reflects greater concerns with reciprocity and equality among individuals. Basically, Blatt and Kohlberg allow students at adjacent stages of moral development to argue with each other about a number of moral dilemmas. About half of the students at the lower stage move up, while virtually none of the higher stage children move down.

Intentionality is embedded in these types of psychological education. Training in achievement motivation, human relations skills and moral development all represent specific commitments to provide individuals with what they need to make their own choices. All of these curricula are based on research and conceptual frameworks showing that individuals who receive such training will be better prepared to live effectively after school. Finally, we all can hope that when students have learned to choose their own goals and attain those goals through a sequence of alternative procedures, several other attitudes may emerge: a respect for different viewpoints of others; the ability to live with failures and persist until goals are reached; and the self-confidence and self-esteem that result from succeeding.

References

Aldridge, E. The Microteaching Paradigm in the Instruction of Junior High School Students in Attending Behavior. Unpublished doctoral dissertation, Amherst: University of Massachusetts, 1971.

Alschuler, A.S. *Developing Achievement Motivation in Adolescents*. Englewood Cliffs, New Jersey: Educational Technology Publications, Inc., 1973.

Alschuler, A.S., D. Tabor and J. McIntyre. *Teaching Achievement Motivation.* Middletown, Connecticut: Education Ventures, Inc., 1970.

Blatt, M. and L. Kohlberg. The Effects of Classroom Discussion Programs Upon the Moral Levels of Pre-Adolescents. *Merrill Palmer Quarterly,* 1970.

Coleman, J. *Equality of Educational Opportunity*. USOE OE38001, Washington, D.C.: Government Printing Office, 1966.

Elkind, D. Piagetian and Psychometric Conceptions of Intelligence. *Harvard Educational Review,* 1969, 39, 319-337.

Hoyt, D.P. The Relationship Between College Grades and Adult Achievement: A Review of the Literature. *American College Testing Program Research Reports,* 1965, 7, 1-58.

Husen, T. *International Study of Achievement in Mathematics*. Vol. 2. Uppsala, Sweden: Almquist and Wiksellsi, 1967.

Ivey, A. The Intentional Individual: A Process-Outcome View of Behavioral Psychology. *The Counseling Psychologist,* 1969, 1, 56-60.

Ivey, A. *Microcounseling: Innovations in Interviewing Training.* Springfield, Illinois: C.C. Thomas, 1972.

Ivey, A., C. Normington, C. Miller, W. Morrill and R. Hasse. Microcounseling and Attending Behavior: An Approach to Pre-Practicum Counselor Training. *Journal of Counseling Psychology,* 1968, 15, 1-12.

Ivey, A. and S. Rollin. A Behavioral Objectives Curriculum in Teacher Education. *Journal of Teacher Education,* 1971.

Kirschenbaum, H., S.B. Simon and R. Napier. *Wad-ja-get.* New York: Hart Publishing Company, 1971.

Kohlberg, L., J. La Cross and D. Ricks. The Predictability of Adult Mental Health from Childhood Behavior. In *Handbook of Child Psychopathology.* New York: McGraw-Hill, 1970.

McClelland, D.C. and D.G. Winter. *Motivating Economic Achievement.* New York: Free Press, 1969.

Moreland, J. Video Programmed Instruction in Elementary Psychotherapeutic and Related Clinical Skills. Unpublished doctoral dissertation, Amherst: University of Massachusetts, 1971.

Rollin, S. The Development and Testing of a Performance Curriculum in Human Relations. Unpublished doctoral dissertation, Amherst: University of Massachusetts, 1970.

17

Competency-Based Education and the Open Classroom

Frances Rice

Traditionally, students have been grouped in classrooms according to age. They have been expected to achieve at the same rate and arrive for the next level of understanding at the same time, usually at the end of an academic year. Classes have been conducted with the teacher directing the content while students listen, speaking only when given permission to do so. Many educators abhor this method of grouping and teaching on the basis that it violates newer theories of learning and does not capitalize on the unique learning capabilities or individualities of students. Various methods have been suggested for rectifying the situation. Some have been experiments with non-graded schools, ability grouping, team teaching, flexible scheduling, non-directive classrooms and the open classroom.

There are as many variations to the open classroom as there are people conducting them; however, there are common elements characteristic to each. The open classroom operates on the assumption that the learner will learn better, enjoy it more, develop behaviors that will enable him to function more effectively in the future when materials are geared to his level of competency, and when he can study at his own rate, and make decisions regarding his learning.

Competency-based learning is based on behavioral objectives; that is, *a priori* behaviors are defined for students. This practice is typical of those open classrooms where objectives are provided in

Frances Rice is at the University of Texas at El Paso.

such curriculum designs as learning activity packages, contracts and modules. In some instances, the objectives are set by teachers or professional educators, and in other instances, behavioral contracts are set by the student. The evaluation of the student's achievement is obtained by criterion-referenced testing, that is, tests designed to determine the achievement of the student's behavior against a standard set by the objective. This type of evaluation is in contrast to norm-referenced testing, usually given in traditional classrooms, in which the test is designed to rank individuals by an established norm. The main concern in the open classroom is not in comparing individuals, but in judging an *individual's* behavior in relation to some standard.

Ever since the open classroom made its way from Britain to America, the open approach to education has proved to be valuable in many ways and has grown in popularity in various sections of the United States. Not all, of course, are competency-based open classrooms (in fact, many "open educators" are critical of behavioral objectives).

It should be noted that by proposing such an innovation as the competency-based open classroom, one is not tendering a panacea for all the ills in our present educational training. Many people feel that the only justification for a method of teaching is that students learn better (more efficiently) and are therefore better prepared to cope effectively in their environment. This implies that, however one feels with respect to the traditional scheme, some students who use it learn better and are better prepared to cope with life's problems. For this reason, there will still be a need for the traditional type of instruction. The open classroom, which is competency-based, is presented here as an alternative method of learning for those with whom it works best.

An Example of an Approach to a Competency-Based Open Classroom

There are many variations in the operation of the open classroom. It is beyond the scope of this chapter to include them all here. Therefore, an example demonstrating the basic characteristics of the competency-based open classroom will be presented.

To illustrate this example, a sample of the activities of a hypothetical student as he moves through a few days in a course are described.

Before we take our student through a class, it is appropriate to set the stage for his performance.

The basic difference between the traditional school and the open classroom is one of organization. In the traditional classroom, the teacher is the center of instruction. Her desk is usually at the front of the room with rows of 30 or 40 desks arranged neatly facing it. The teacher directs an already prescribed curriculum and does most of the talking and demonstrating. In contrast, the furniture in the open classroom might be placed anywhere around the room. The teacher's desk may be placed against the wall and used as a resource center. Other desks may be arranged in a circle or facing each other in clusters of 3 or 4. Usually the room is broken up into learning area centers, each one representing a particular aspect of the curriculum. One center may feature language, with others featuring math, science, social studies and so on. One center may be devoted strictly to interdisciplinary interests, where students may study a particular item of interest not necessarily related to the direction of the basic curriculum. In the competency-based open classroom, the sequence of the curriculum is frequently not as fixed as in the traditional class. The instructional material is usually prepared in the form of learning packages, such as contracts, assignments, activity packages or modules. A student can select the curricular elements in any sequence, making his own judgments about whether or not he can handle them. There is a variety of learning materials—books, pamphlets, tape recorders, films, filmstrips, programmed texts and instructional packages—from which the student may select.

David will be the hypothetical student. He has just arrived for the first day of school. The teacher begins telling the students about how the class will be conducted for the year. He tells them about the learning area centers and that each one is devoted to a particular subject. He explains that although the students are required to complete a certain amount of work satisfactorily before entering high school, they are allowed to work at their own speed and encouraged to work on materials they can understand. The teacher tells the class that they can decide when and if to study, and he and the aide will give help if asked. David learns that by passing a pretest he can receive credit for knowledge he already has, without additional study. David also learns that if he does not take the pretest, he can get credit for learning the material by passing a posttest. He can take the posttest anytime—as often as he desires, until his score on it is passing. The class is informed that there will be no grades such as A, B, C or F. The information reported to parents will be only a record of the work completed, generally a description of the behaviors acquired through the learning processes. The teacher then proceeds to take the learners to the centers, later explaining the modules, activity packages and learning contracts, where to find resource materials, how to use the instructional machines, and how to keep their own learning and testing records. The students are told how to keep the materials orderly and in good condition. After this explanation, the class is informed that they are free to move about and talk, but not to disturb other learners. The class is then left on their own. For the first few days, the teacher and aide are very busy answering questions. Getting off "on the right foot" is very important to the effective operation of the class.

David

David spotted an area in science that he felt he would like to study. He chose "Plankton: Great Pastures of the Ocean." From the file he pulled the assignment page covering Plankton. On this sheet he put his name and the date. This assignment had the following components:
1. Objectives
2. Rationale
3. Pretest
4. Alternative learning activities
5. Instructions
6. Study questions
7. Posttest
8. Resources
He read the objective from the sheet, which is "to have a basic

understanding" of ocean ecology so that he can:

   a. Diagram the basic food sources in the ocean.
   b. Describe factors influencing the food chain.

After reading the instructions and the 20 study questions, David asked the teacher to give him the pretest, which he did not pass. He returned to the assignment and read the list of activities from which he could select for study. Each activity should assist David in understanding something about foods in the ocean and factors influencing the food chain. Below are examples of these activities:

   1. Film: "Plankton: Pastures of the Ocean"
   2. Film Loops: "Oceans and Seas"
   3. Transparencies: "Cycle of Life in the Ocean"
   4. Research in Encyclopedia
   5. Group research and discussion
   6. Lecture
   7. Read *The Sea*. Learner, Engel and the Editors of Time-Life, Inc. New York, 1961.

David selected No. 7, *The Sea*, and found a quiet place to read. He tried to study but found he could not concentrate. Seeing a friend who appeared to have the same problem, David approached him and asked if he would like to play a game. Then both went over to the interest center, selected a game and commenced playing. The teacher paid no attention. They played about an hour; then, David, feeling that he should study, but still unable to concentrate on *The Sea* or science, selected another contract, on reading comprehension. The story he selected to read was of immediate interest to him and he began to read; but school was almost over for the day.

Tuesday, David felt more inclined to study science. He had taken the reading book home, but found it too sophisticated for him to understand. He decided to change to the encyclopedia for research and began studying. From his encyclopedia reading, he became interested in some facts about the sea and shared them with a couple of his friends. This started a conversation and soon two of his friends were reading the encyclopedia and talking about what they found there. When the other two boys lost interest, David started answering the study questions and completed them all. After a brief study period, he asked the teacher to let him take the posttest. The teacher sent him to a quiet place and gave him the test. After David had completed the test, the teacher quickly graded the test, marking the correct responses. David missed a point in his diagram and 2 points in describing factors influencing the food chain. In the following conference, the teacher asked David about his questionable answers. He found that David really had been wrong about the diagram item, and had misinterpreted the question in one instance and failed to express himself effectively about one of the food chain factors. After (and because of) probing and questioning David about his test performance, the teacher recorded a "pass" on David's test and told him how well he did. The teacher then entered the date of completion on the assignment sheet and placed it in David's file. David then went to his file and recorded a "pass" and the date completed in his posttest record. He was ready now for the next assignment.

If David had failed the test, he would have had to go back to study the material he had been studying, or he could have selected an alternate learning activity in preparation for his second try at the posttest. This "recycling" process could be repeated several times. Repeated inability to complete the posttest satisfactorily would have been of concern to David's teacher, and, on his request, appropriate counseling would have ensued. If his trouble had been the reading or comprehension, he could have gone to the teacher for help in clarifying concepts, defining words, or developing reading skills.

For this entire day, David worked on science. His next assignment was "The Life Zones in the Ocean." He made no attempt at the pretest, but began studying. This time he selected a filmstrip labeled "Oceanography—Understanding Our Deep Frontier."

Even though there were many days when David chose not to work in science, he did concentrate, the last few weeks of school, on his science studies and completed what corresponded to a year's work. As for the remaining subjects, language, social studies, mathematics, etc., the work went very much the same. David selected what, when and how he wanted to study. He selected materials (sometimes through trial and error) that fitted his learning style, level of achievement and interest.

The Teacher's Role

The teacher's role working in an open classroom is less one of being the central figure than in a traditional class. He is a diagnostician and as such prepares materials to suit the various learning styles of the individual students. He is a tutor and an advisor, but only when asked by the student. He works cooperatively and closely with the students, and with other teachers and administrators in acquiring materials and revising dysfunctional ones. His attitude always is one of finding solutions to problems rather than assigning blame for what has not been done. He is an evaluator, scoring tests promptly when they have been completed, and keeps records and files of the work of each student.

The Student's Role

The student's role in an open classroom is one of responsibility for his learning. He decides what, when, how and if he will study. He is responsible for seeking help if he needs it. This help can come from the teachers or from peers through exchanging of ideas, asking questions, or exploring each other's views. He is to respect the rights of others and work cooperatively with students, teachers and administrators. In some open classrooms, the students are expected to keep their own records up-to-date and file them. Competency is achieved by allowing the learner to define attainable behaviors and standards as they pertain to his unique concept of *his education.*

Problems to Consider

The competency-based open classroom is not exactly a magic or blemish-free learning situation. It has its problems and drawbacks. One problem is finding teachers who are "sold" on the idea and able to work effectively with it. Another is finding teachers adequately trained to diagnose individual learning difficulties and learning styles. It is also difficult for teachers to become familiar with the resource materials and the amounts of knowledge in the diverse subject fields which may be presented in a single classroom. Finding time for staff planning is difficult. Resources are a problem, as well as the financial sources for their acquisition. There is also the matter of keeping up with the numerous records that must be kept, and finally the problem of maintenance of instructional hardware—film projectors, tape recorders, etc.

Summary

Competency-based education in the open classroom is a flexible strategy to enhance long-life learning and a person's self-concept. The approaches to the open concept are many and varied; however, there is a strain of common elements running through them.

The competency-based open classroom is based on objectives which have been previously set by teachers or professional educators and/or by the student himself. The open classroom is non-authoritarian. There is opportunity for interaction among all persons involved in the program and opportunity for learning to high standards. Students are responsible for their learning and learn to decide when to study. They can select activities which fit their learning style. Pretesting and posttesting are practiced. Posttesting is on learner demand and may be repeated an indefinite number of times. The students should be evaluated on individual progress rather than group norms.

The open concept is not free from difficulties. Teachers must be proficient in many areas, and at present adequately trained personnel are difficult to find. Money is a factor, since the open classroom requires many materials and supplies, and maintenance of hardware. However, in the long run, cost effectiveness of open classrooms may be competitive with traditional methods of learning.

18

Implications of Competency-Based Education for Urban Children

Leon M. Lessinger

If I had to say which was telling the truth about society,
a speech by a minister of housing or the actual buildings
put up in his time, I should believe the buildings.
Kenneth Clark in *Civilisation.*

Competency-based education begins by challenging basic assumptions. It strikes at a set of traditional beliefs which are at the center of educational dogma: (1) the mastery of a certain body of knowledge is the essence of education; (2) creating a succession of hurdles within a competitive system and requiring students to demonstrate *both* mastery of certain knowledge and willingness to exert effort toward a formal, if not necessarily relevant, goal ensures that only intelligent and dedicated individuals rise to the top; and (3) people are distributed along a normal curve, and it is necessary to assess a person's aptitude to certify his admissability into the total program of gaining mastery of certain bodies of knowledge. Coffman (1969) shows this belief in action in his review of the 3,000-year history of civil service examinations in Imperial China. He points out:

The parallel to the requirement of a college degree for
entry into many positions at the present time will not
be lost on the alert observer. Often it is not the
particular knowledge required by an examination or
implied by a diploma but rather the ability to acquire

Leon M. Lessinger, former Associate U.S. Commissioner of Education, is
Dean of the School of Education, University of South Carolina.

new knowledge implicit in the examination grade or in the degree that marks the individual as competent to undertake a new responsibility. Thus where the selection ratio is low, an inefficient and irrelevant educational system may nevertheless provide a means of screening out the required leadership.

Such thinking, widely supported though it may be, survives as a relic with unfortunate effects upon education in the urban setting. Probably the main implication of competency-based education for urban children is its revision of the traditional thinking about aptitude—the keystone in the dogma discussed.

Competency-based education does not negate the fact that students differ in their aptitude for learning; it simply presents aptitude as a function of the amount of time and resource needed to attain an operationalized description of competence, not as the degree of mastery attained in a given program during a given time. Obviously, some students become competent more quickly than others. What matters most with regard to a stipulated competency is not how long a child took to gain it or the type of training he received, but the fact that he now can perform. The rest is a matter of economics.

From the very beginning, American schools reflected the goals and principles of the young frontier society. The set of small-sized enterprises turned out students to fill what were essentially limited education needs of a developing nation. The vast majority of students were processed by the schools for unskilled work on farms and in factories. By a reject process of screening and sorting around content largely irrelevant to the needs of the majority, the schools permitted a small number of students (supposedly those with the most potential) to progress to the highest grades to carry on the culture in the colleges and professions. Demand for highly educated citizens was low, the concept of a drop-out was unknown, and the low school productivity was quite in keeping with the markets then available.

The schools of America did indeed respond to our national needs. They responded, at least, until the population and accompanying technological explosions of World War II and its aftermath changed the nature of the nation's demands on the schools. Sputniks and crowded cities, computers and confrontation politics, television and black power and a fundamental change in the rate of change—all have placed new and overwhelming demands on our old educational system. What we must answer now is a set of new questions: how to provide the kind of education that assures full participation for all in this new urban, complex, technological society; how to prepare our people to respond creatively to rapid-fire change all their lives while maintaining a personal identity that can give them and the society purpose and direction; how to do this when the body of knowledge has so exploded that it can no longer be stored in a single mind; how to do this when the cost of old-fashioned education soars higher year by year without significantly improving; how to do this with an institution which like all institutions is effectively resistant to change.

Competency-based education is clearly a response to such concerns. A little history may be useful at this point.

In 1947, the President's Commission on Higher Education called for a program which would equalize educational opportunities for all young Americans. In the spring of 1954, the U.S. Supreme Court handed down the decision, in *Brown vs. Board of Education,* that "separate education facilities are inherently unequal." Said the Court: "In these days, it is doubtful that any child may reasonably be expected to succeed in life if he is denied the opportunity of an education. Such an opportunity, where the state has undertaken to provide it, is a right which must be made available to all on equal terms."

Not until 1965, however, and the passage of the far-reaching Elementary and Secondary Education Act "to strengthen and improve educational quality and educational opportunities in the nation's schools," did the public schools of America get a clear new mandate and some of the funds to carry it out. Equity of accomplishment was to replace screening and sorting. The new goal for education, established by the legislation of 1965, was to be competence for all.

In place of the old screening, sorting and reject system that put students on the bell-shaped probability curve from A to F, the schools were now asked to prepare every young person for a productive life. Under the old system, a fourth to a third of all students automatically went to the bottom of the barrel. Under the new mandate, the schools were asked to give every pupil the competence he needs, regardless of so-called ability, interest, background, home or income.* In effect, said the nation: "What's the purpose of grading a basic skill like reading with A, B, C, D or F when you can't make it at all today if you can't read?"

All human institutions exist to provide products or services to human beings. An essential aspect of these products or services is that they be fit for use. This phrase "fitness for use" is the basic meaning of the word "quality."** In education, the mark of quality therefore is fitness: an apt synonym for competence.

What, in fact, the nation began to demand in 1965 then was a "zero reject system" for education—one which increases the quality, i.e., fitness, of each child much as the zero defect system improves the quality of spaceship production. The nation asked that the results of schooling be a learner, who will meet at least minimum performance criteria before leaving the school system.

As long ago as 1907, Teddy Roosevelt preached the idea of trained-minds-in-trained-bodies that must flower in the last decades of this century if all the children of all the people are to be educated to their fullest potential. For at least 100 years the rhetoric of education has centered on seven separate training goals. The first, *intellectual discipline,* has been debated only in terms of how the ideal of "mind training" or "critical thinking" was to have been achieved. The second, *economic independence,* received its major thrust from Benjamin Franklin. That he was "keenly disappointed" in the progress toward this goal and that the

---

*Socrates is made to reflect the typical obsessive educational concern with student "potential" in an amusing way. He says, "Now, then, tell me something about yourself. The information is essential if I'm to know what strategies to employ against you."

**See Juran, J.M. and Frank M. Gryna, Jr. *Quality Planning and Analysis.* New York: McGraw-Hill, 1970, for an extensive discussion of this theme.

disappointment continues to this day, as shown in the revived concern for career education, merely stresses its importance.

Citizenship and civic responsibility is a recurrent theme. The third goal receives major emphasis in over ninety percent of the statutes enacted concerning goals for the public schools in the United States.

A fourth goal, *social development and human relationships,* was first directly recorded as a goal in the famous "Seven Cardinal Objectives of Education." While there are differences in emphasis and points-of-view on how this goal should be achieved, most states would have their youth achieve "acceptable social skills."

The fifth goal, *morals and ethical character,* began as a goal in the religious training of the colonial era. It evolved to the concept of disciplined ways of "thinking, feeling and acting," and to their restatement by the Commission on Imperatives in Education in 1966 as " . . . to strengthen the moral fabric of society."

The goal of *self-realization*, a sixth purpose, has been vigorously pursued. This has ranged from the "rugged-individualism" characteristics of the founders and pioneers to the present emphasis on seeking "personal identity" and a wholesome "self-image." The goal has included ideas of self-reliance achieved through the individual capability to communicate, calculate, be self-directive and demonstrate esthetic and intellectual interests. More recently, ideas involving good mental and emotional health have been included.

Finally, there is the traditional concern with the *physical well-being and accomplishment* of the person as a major goal.

In concept, then, education exists to provide the training that is expected to produce capable, competent and skilled citizens. Seen from the historical perspective of goal development, it is hardly surprising that the notion of competence or fitness is also synonymous with such words as "suitable," "happy," "proper," "appropriate," "apt" and "felicitous." Seen from this same perspective it *is* surprising that training is generally unenthusiastically embraced by educators. A second major contribution of competence as the central concern of the schools is its association with training.

The rediscovery of the centrality of training to education bears further exploration. In a series of papers Carkhuff has synthesized an impressive array of research to provide substance to this conclusion. Using the techniques of systematic observation pioneered by Flanders and others, along with the quantification of such human relations constructs as *empathy, genuineness, confrontation, nonpossessive-warmth* and *unconditional positive regard,* Carkhuff has shown that building competency by systematically training the student and the significant others (teachers, parents, etc.) in his environment gives evidence of positive growth toward academic, social, humane and vocational goals. As Carkhuff (1971) has written,

the number of unique benefits of systematic training as education may be summarized as follows:

1. systematic training is goal-directed and action-oriented;

2. systematic training emphasizes practice in the behavior which we wish to effect;

3. systematic training leaves the trainees with tangible and useable skills;

4. systematic training promotes longer retention of learned skills;

5. systematic training enables us to make systematic selection of trainees; and

6. systematic training offers a built-in means for assessing the effectiveness of the program.

Thus far, we have emphasized training as a necessary precondition of education. Simply stated, systematic training of teachers prepared them more effectively for discharging their functions than non-systematic preparation. In this vein, we may conclude that the more systematic the teacher's preparation for all spheres is functioning the more effective the teacher. Further, we may extend this to say that those ways in which the teacher learns most effectively are also the ways in which the student learns most effectively. In conclusion, the more we know about what we are doing,

the more we are conducting training rather than what
we have traditionally conceived of as education.

With competency as the cluster of operationalized objectives
under the seven goals of intellectual, economic, civic, ethical,
social, self and physical fitness and systematic training as one of
the major means, the basis for accountability is established. What
are some important other implications of competency-based
education for the urban setting?

With competency as a goal, we can build a comprehensive
educational program properly relating the school as a system to
the societal system within which it must be relevantly embedded.
For so many of our urban youth, the school experience is totally
unlike the life they know and non-useful in helping them achieve
the life they need. Like the civil service personnel of Imperial
China already alluded to, they move through a succession of
hurdles within a competitive system requiring candidates to
demonstrate ability to acquire bodies of knowledge of value to a
select few.

What we must do is to use both the school setting and the
community setting as places to gain and practice competency. This
can be done by getting young people out of the classrooms and
into the real world and bringing adults into the classroom. Thus
we must place our young people to work in hospitals and
orphanages, in community centers and adult continuation schools,
in offices and factories and laboratories. We need to get young
people serving each other in the schools, and in after-school
study-tutorial centers. We need to permit and encourage students
to use a teacher, an adult—or, as often, a teaching machine or
other mediated instruction. We ought to see in the classrooms,
parents, lawyers, doctors, photographers, housewives, builders,
labor union leaders, students from nearby colleges and business-
men—all contributing realism and knowledge of the need for and
use of competent people.

This is, of course, a description of a performance curriculum
embedded in the real world. Such an approach provides a
profound change in the nature of formal education. It recognizes
the pitfalls of urban schools separated from life. It spreads to the

schools and classrooms the spirit of theater rehearsals, the playing field, orchestra practice, the lab and business seminar, the world of work. It is a vision of young people handling data and problems from the real world as well as from carefully contrived experiments taken from major job families. It is an educational system producing and being accountable for "fitness for use"—a young citizenry competent to be voters, family members, technicians, artists and market analysts, and, yes, competent in the skills necessary to live the good life and to pursue happiness.

Such an educational system, organized around demonstrated competence, would emphasize—in addition to systematic training—systematic management and systematic renewal. No student in a system like this would be rejected if he could not perform. He would be worked with, placed in special learning situations, instructed individually until, over varying time, *he could succeed.* In this way an accountable society would assure that each person had what he must have to function in a free and dynamic society. For our urban children, this would be good news indeed.

References

Carkhuff, Robert R. Training as a Necessary Pre-Condition of Education: The Development and Generalization of a Systematic Resource Training Model. *Journal of Research and Development in Education.* Winter 1971, *4* (2), 12-13.

Coffman, William E. Achievement Tests. In *Encyclopedia of Educational Research*, Fourth Edition. New York: The Macmillan Company, 1969.

19

A Review of the Research on
Performance-Based Teacher Education

Joel L. Burdin
and Moira B. Mathieson

The concept of performance-based teacher education (PBTE) is relatively new, and although there are a number of papers dealing with it, they consist mainly of opinions, discussions and descriptions. They report very little research on PBTE or its companion term of "competency."

This chapter pulls together a sampling of research to indicate what has been done and to suggest needed detailed research in the future.

Hanushek (No. 7 below) claims that it is easier to analyze results of education than methods of improving it. "It is surprising how little is actually known about the ways in which schools and teachers affect education. This largely results from a fixation on inputs to education rather than outputs." Some question whether it is even possible to measure teacher competence:

> It is unfortunate that the results of sixty years of research have not been commensurate with the expenditure of time and effort. They have, in fact, been conflicting and inconclusive to a degree that has led many otherwise rational members of the profession to a defeatist inference that teacher competence cannot be measured. It is difficult to reconcile this verdict with the fact that many major functions in education depend on the assumption that teacher competence is both variable and measurable (No. 15 below).

Joel L. Burdin is Director and **Moira B. Mathieson** is Senior Information Analyst, ERIC Clearinghouse for Teacher Education.

Fourteen annotated citations make up the main body of this chapter. They represent serious attempts to clarify PBTE. Some conclusions recur several times, particularly that teacher education should be individualized and that internships are among the most important aspects of preparing educational personnel. There follows a bibliography, with a brief description of the research program and a more detailed description of the results, frequently in the author's own words. Each document except Number 14 is available on microfiche in the ERIC collection, so that anyone interested in a more complete account of the research has easy access to the original document through ERIC (and often from the original source). Ordering information is provided in each issue of *Research in Education (RIE)*, the basic abstract journal of the U.S. Office of Education.

The three final entries do not include research results and call for some additional comment. Items 15 and 16 are included as sources for additional material. Item 17 is a bibliography prepared by the American Association of Colleges for Teacher Education in collaboration with the ERIC Clearinghouse for Teacher Education. It includes much of the existing material on performance-based teacher education and is therefore of importance to anyone wishing to learn more about the development and definition of the concept, and the ways in which it is being implemented.

One who wishes to expand this bibliography through the ERIC system should use the following "descriptors" or search terms:

"Teacher Education"
"Performance Criteria"
"Educational Accountability"
"Evaluation Criteria"
"Performance Factors"
"Academic Achievement"

To use a descriptor: (1) Look up the descriptor in the SUBJECT INDEX of monthly, semi-annual or annual issues of *RIE*. (2) Beneath the descriptors you will find title(s) of documents. Decide which title(s) you wish to pursue. (3) Note the ED number beside the title. (4) Look up the ED number in the

DOCUMENT RESUME SECTION of the appropriate issue of *RIE*. With the number you will find a summary of the document and often the document's cost in microfiche and/or hardcopy. (5) Repeat the above procedure, if desired, for other issues of *RIE* and other descriptors. (6) For information about how to order ERIC documents, turn to the back pages of *RIE*. (7) Indexes and annotations of journal articles can be found in *Current Index to Journals in Education* by following the same procedure. Periodical articles cannot be secured through ERIC.

1.   Berry, John R. *Professional Preparation and Effectiveness of Beginning Teachers.* Coral Gables, Florida: University of Miami, 1960. 90 p., ED 052 156.

    This study, carried out in 1959-60 in the public schools of three counties in southeastern Florida, compared the teaching effectiveness of beginning teachers who are provisionally certified because of lack of all or some of the prescribed preparation in education courses with teachers who have met full certification requirements. There were 76 teachers in each of the two groups. Systematic and repeated classroom observations were used to estimate teaching effectiveness, with each teacher observed five times during the year. Each teacher was also rated twice by his principal. The original item ratings from the Classroom Observation Report (adopted by the one developed by Ryan for the American Council on Education) were converted into standard scores, which in turn were averaged to give five subscores which formed the basic data for analysis. The following findings were reported:

    "(1) On the basis of systematic classroom observation, the fully certified beginning teachers who had completed the prescribed courses in education were consistently and significantly rated by competent observers to be more effective than the provisionally certified teachers who lacked all or part of the sequence in education courses.

    "(2) The differences in rating on teaching effectiveness were associated with differences in professional preparation rather than with differences in background factors such as grades in college, amount of work in the subject taught, interview scores, age, or recency of graduation.

    "(3) The observers from professional fields other than education recognized the superiority of the fully prepared teachers to about the same degree that the educator observers did.

    "(4) The correlations between age and recency of graduation and the effectiveness subscores for the secondary teachers were slight but consistently positive; for the elementary teachers, slight but consistently negative.

    "(5) Although the fully certified teachers as a group were rated more effective than the provisionally certified teachers as a group, there was overlapping in the two distributions, and some provisionally certified teachers were rated higher than some fully certified ones.

"(6) Although the study was not set up to get comparable ratings from the principals as it was to get comparable ratings from the observers, where principals' ratings were available in equal number from provisionally and fully certified teachers assigned to the same school, the mean ratings favored the fully certified teachers, but not sufficiently so to be statistically significant."

2.   Borg, Walter R. *The Minicourse as a Vehicle for Changing Teacher Behavior. The Research Evidence.* Paper presented at the annual meeting of the American Educational Research Association, February 1969, Los Angeles. 14 p., ED 029 809.

This research was intended to test the effectiveness of the minicourse (an instructional microteaching package) in changing specific teacher behaviors. Twenty-minute pre- and post-minicourse videotaped recordings of 48 participating teachers' classroom lessons were made and scored by trained raters. Results of a posttest administered two months later indicated that the teachers had retained most of the skills acquired in the minicourse without the need for a refresher course.

While both groups made substantial gains on most of the behaviors measured, teachers serving predominantly lower-class areas made greater gains on most of the skills than those teachers serving predominantly middle-class areas. No significant differences were found in the gains made by male versus female teachers or in their retention of the skills four months after completion of the course.

The author comments: "If you compare the teachers' performance means on the pre-course video tapes and the delayed post-course video tapes, I believe you will agree that the degree to which most of these behaviors improved is striking. Consider, for example, the reductions in three behaviors that Minicourse I attempts to extinguish. The average teacher repeated his own questions 14 times in the 20-minute, pre-course lesson. This behavior was reduced to a bit over two times for the average teacher on the delayed post-course lesson. Equally dramatic reductions occurred in the number of times teachers repeated pupil answers and the number of times they answered their own questions. Also note that the proportion of higher cognitive versus fact questions was nearly doubled while proportion of teacher talk was nearly halved between the pre-course and delayed post-course lessons."

3.   Briet, Frank and David P. Butts. *A Comparison of the Effectiveness of an Inservice Program and Preservice Program in Developing Certain Teacher Competencies.* Paper presented at a meeting of the National Association for Research in Science Teaching, February 1969, Pasadena, California. 15 p., ED 028 069.

"The major purpose of this study was to examine the relative effectiveness of a teacher education program given at the preservice level and at the inservice level in the development of certain teaching competencies related to successful implementation of a curriculum innovation." The results of the study indicate that the total experience was successful in developing knowledge of the processes of science and changing instructional decision behavior of both preservice participants and inservice participants. The close similarity in pretest scores between the treatment groups and their respective no-treatment groups and the high level of significance of the differences in gain scores allows for considerable confidence in this conclusion.

"It was found that the total experience did affect attitude but only to a limited extent . . . The changes in attitude noted seem to indicate that the total experience had a bigger impact on the inservice participants. This could be due to the nature of an inservice program. For many teachers participation in an inservice program is a welcome break in the daily routine. On the other hand, the preservice version of the program is simply one of a number of courses taken by the participants. It is also possible that the change in attitude toward the program is related to how relevant the participants see the program (to be). Inservice participants, having taught, can perhaps see a greater need for the type of help offered by a teacher education program.

"Both preservice participants and inservice participants made substantial change in their instruction decision behavior. The preservice participants began at a significantly higher level than the inservice participants and retained this difference at the end of the program. This could indicate that the aspects of the program which dealt with instructional decision behavior were of equal benefit to individuals at various levels of competence and with or without teaching experience.

"In general, it was concluded that preservice and inservice teachers who experience a similar teacher education program exhibit some similar changes and some contrasting changes. Further study of these changes seems to support the conclusion that teacher education programs need to be constructed to meet the differing needs of the participants."

4.   Clegg, Ambrose A. and Anna Ochoa. *Evaluation of a Performance-Based Program in Teacher Education: Recommendations for Implementation.* Seattle: University of Washington, College of Education, August 1970. 80 p., ED 057 017.

The Experimental Model for Teacher Education was implemented during the academic year 1969-70. Its major objective was to build a field-based program using predefined behavioral objectives and their accompanying performance criteria with an instructional program integrating theoretical knowledge with practical experience. Twenty trainees were selected for the program on the basis of grade-point average and a personal

interview. Administrative arrangements were made to allow program participants to take their professional courses on a pass-fail basis. Seminars were
coordinated with concurrent classroom experience at progressively increasing
levels of responsibility in three types of school: inner city, urban and
suburban. Cooperating teachers in these schools were designated "clinical
associates" and provided with inservice training. Of the 20 trainees, 17
completed the program successfully and were certified. Of these, 12 had
obtained teaching positions as of June, 1970. Detailed recommendations for
program improvement include closer involvement of cooperating schools,
previous rather than concurrent training of clinical associates, and involvement of trainees in developing objectives and criteria.

"It appears that performance-based programs may place additional
demands on prospective teachers. Since some considerable effort was made to
select candidates who appeared to have a higher probability of success in
teaching, the 15 percent attrition rate may reflect that such programs are
more rigorous and demanding than traditional preparation. Additionally, for
some individuals, the constraints of performance criteria pose an insurmount-
able barrier."

5.   Cooper, James G. and Katherine A. Bemis. *Teacher Personality, Teacher
      Behavior, and Their Effects Upon Pupil Achievement.* Final Report.
      Albuquerque: University of New Mexico, College of Education, April
      1967. 156 p., ED 012 707.

Sixty urban, middle-class, fourth-grade teachers in the Southwest were
given the Edwards Personal Preference Schedule (EPPS) as a measure of
personality. Their classroom behavior was then recorded on a Teacher
Observation Personality Schedule reflecting Edwards' definitions of need for
achievement, abasement, affiliation, dominance, change, orderliness and
heterosexuality. Pupils' achievement was measured as their adjusted gain
scores between fall and spring testing on five subtests of the Science Research
Associates achievement tests. It was found that: (1) no single teacher
behavior was detrimental or favorable for all learning; (2) the EPPS scores
established a basis for predicting teachers' observed classroom behavior; (3)
the pattern of predicted behaviors did not follow closely that revealed as
contributing to pupil gains; and (4) from EPPS, the more effective teachers
(in terms of pupil gains) may be described as critical, willing to accept
leadership and interested in persuading and influencing others.

The study validated the Medley-Mitzel model for studying teacher
effectiveness. "Their postulated three major linkages: *teacher personality*
causes *teacher behavior* causes *pupil behavior,* have been supported.
But . . . the linkages are not one-to-one; they are complex relations. Our data
showed that teachers' classroom behavior is related to adjusted pupil gain.
The Edwards Personal Preference Schedule was found to be related to our

teachers' classroom behaviors, but not in a manner that enabled us to directly predict those behaviors found related to above average pupil gain. The EPPS also provided profiles of a sort that identified those teachers who were more likely to effect higher gains than predicted from their pupils' fall test means."

6. Coyne, Charles E. *Comparative Analysis of Teacher Education.* Final Report. St. Joseph: Missouri Western College, December 1970. 31 p., ED 050 048.

This study was initiated to determine the directions to be taken to train and develop qualified and competent teachers, using experimental and control groups, with a follow-up of on-the-job performance of graduates. The cooperating schools, the association of these in-school experiences with the educational theory and methods of a teacher education program, the uses of videotape and the attitudes and awareness of the graduating teacher were examined.

"An analysis of the results of this study led to several conclusions. As evidenced by the follow-up of all students involved in the study that graduated and chose to teach, any well-planned, purposeful program in teacher education will produce well-skilled and competent teachers.

"It was further concluded that all individuals benefited greatly from their student teaching exposure. It would appear from the data collected that pre-student teaching experiences are valuable in assisting the student in the achievement of maximum performance during student teaching.

"Based on the findings of this limited study, it would appear that an early exposure to the school program and to teaching is helpful in assisting the student in determining his desire to teach, the grade level in which he wishes to teach, and the subject field or level in which he may wish to teach.

"In analyzing the data collected it would appear that courses associated with the in-school involvement are more meaningful, and aid students in the area of perceiving and analyzing classroom situations. Psychological implications appeared to be more related to the behavioral situations and a greater awareness of teaching methodology was indicated."

7. Hanushek, Eric. The Production of Education, Teacher Quality and Efficiency. *Do Teachers Make a Difference? A Report on Recent Research on Pupil Achievement.* Washington, D.C.: Government Printing Office, 1970, pp. 79-99. Publisher's price: $0.75, order number HE 5.258:58042. ED 037 396.

This study examined the educational process to identify teacher role in education and school efficiency in hiring teachers. The implicit educational model used by administrators is known: a teacher's productivity is a function of experience and educational level. A conceptual model of the educational process was developed which states that educational output, itself a multi-dimensional factor, is a function of the cumulative background influences of the individual's family, the influences of his peers, his innate abilities, and the school inputs. Two separate analyses of elementary school processes, based on the model, were undertaken, one relying on data from the Northeast and Great Lakes of the "Equality of Educational Opportunity" survey (713 schools) and one using a sample drawn from a California school district in 1969. Educational output was measured only by achievement tests. Black, white and Mexican-American students were considered separately for part of the study.

"The strongest conclusion from the models is that school systems now operate quite inefficiently. They are buying the wrong attributes of teachers, i.e., attributes which lead to little or no achievement gains. However, it is more difficult to develop the positive side . . . Thus, these models do not provide a practical guide to the school administrator. They only say that there is something there that is desirable for teachers to have.

" . . . some analysis . . . suggests that schools implicitly buy attributes such as teacher verbal facility, (but) buying these through a scale in terms of experience and education cannot help but be inefficient. Further, it is evident through comparing verbal scores for teachers with national norms that present salary schedules do not attract the best college graduates into teaching. However, more information is needed about the supply schedules for specific teacher attributes.

"At the same time it appears to be very important to expand the measures of output. Achievement test scores certainly do not reflect all dimensions of educational output. The relationship among different outputs of education is very imperfectly understood at this point.

" . . . the general low effect of purchased aspects of teachers (advanced education and experience) indicates that schools are acting inefficiently. Since school systems pay handsome bonuses for these attributes, it is only economical to have people with advanced degrees if they contribute a proportionately higher amount to achievement. This does not appear to be the case.

" . . . there is also the distinct impression that teacher quality impacts more on blacks than on whites . . . it would be able to increase black achievement without changing white achievement by shuffling teachers with more experience into predominantly black classrooms (and possibly compensating predominantly white classrooms with more verbal teachers)."

8.   Hoyt, Donald P. *Identifying Effective Teaching Behaviors.* Manhattan: Kansas State University, December 1969. 136 p., ED 039 197.

The major purpose of this study was to determine what specific instructional behaviors, if any, were related to success in teaching. Success was defined in terms of student progress on objectives valued by the instructor.

The findings showed that a number of specific items were related to success (progress) on each objective for both large and small classes. A few items were selected regardless of objectives or size of class; a few others were generally related to success in either small classes or large classes, but not both; and a number were related to success under some conditions (class size, objective) but not others. From these findings, it was concluded that there are some teaching processes which are generally helpful, some others which are helpful with classes of a given size, and others which are helpful when a given objective is stressed. A comprehensive account of effective teaching behaviors appears to require at least 16 somewhat overlapping, yet distinct, descriptions. Some conclusions reached were:

(1) There was evidence that students can make assessments of their progress on specific educational objectives with acceptable validity.

(2) While the quality of instruction and level of student progress tended to be about the same for most of the subgroups studied, there was a consistent advantage for classes taught by the recitation method and for upper-division classes; and small classes were more effective than large in advanced course work.

(3) "Effective teaching procedures" differ depending on size of class and type of objective.

9.   Lawson, Dene R. *Indicators of Teacher Ability to Relate to Students.* Paper presented at the annual meeting of the American Educational Research Association, 1971, New York. 26 p., ED 050 008.

This study attempts to determine the meaning students give to teacher ability to relate to students, and to see if a significant difference exists among scores teachers received from students of differing ethnic backgrounds.

"In general, this investigation determined that students tend to rate higher on ability to relate to students those teachers who: (1) lecture in response to student talk; (2) are not artificially disadvantaged by technical difficulties with sound (this refers to the quality of audio on the videotapes); (3) allow students freedom to initiate discussion; and (4) use praise extensively in rewarding students.

"On the other hand, students tend to rate less favorably . . . those teachers who: (1) permit silence in the classroom to continue for prolonged periods of time; (2) give directions for extended periods of time; (3) prolong an activity; and (4) ask questions for prolonged periods of time.

"To the extent that one might draw conclusions from low but significant correlations, the research finds evidence among the results of this study to substantiate the conjecture that *teacher relatability* is enhanced more by what teachers allow students to do than by what the teacher is doing.

" . . . high school students categorize teachers in similar fashion, regardless of ethnic group or sex of student."

10. Sandefur, J.T. and others. *An Experimental Study of Professional Education for Secondary Teachers.* Final Report. Emporia: Kansas State Teachers College, July 1967, 150 p., ED 022 724.

This study was designed to compare the behavior of 52 secondary education students in a conventional program with that of 62 students in an experimental program, which coordinated laboratory experiences of observation and participation with selected readings and seminars in the foundation areas of psychology, philosophy and anthropology.

The specific objectives of investigation were (1) to identify and organize knowledge related to teaching and learning in a systematic fashion, (2) to design and implement a series of laboratory experiences to accompany the professional content and thereby eliminate the traditional lag between theory and practice, (3) to incorporate both the content and companion laboratory experiences into a new design for the presentation of professional education and to test experimentally the new design against the traditional course offerings in terms of consequent teacher behavior. The following main conclusions were reached:

1. There was a significant difference in the teaching behavior of students enrolled in the control program as measured by independent observers using the Classroom Observation Record. The experimental group received the more desirable behavior ratings.

2. There was a significant difference in the behavior of the pupils of both the experimental and control students as measured by independent observers using the Classroom Observation Record. The more desirable behavior ratings were given to the pupils of the experimental teachers.

3. There was a significant difference in the teaching patterns of the experimental and the control students as measured by independent observers using a sixteen category system of interaction analysis. The experimental group was found to use significantly more indirect activity.

4. Grades earned in student teaching were significantly higher for the experimental students than were those of the control students.

5. Significantly higher scores were made on the Professional Education section of the National Teachers Examination by the control students than were made by the experimental students.

The data examined in this study provided no evidence that the possession of factual information about the professional content of teacher education was sufficient to alter teacher behavior. In fact, evidence to the contrary was indicated in that the students of the control group learned more facts as measured by the National Teachers Examination than did those of the experimental group. Yet their teaching behavior tended to be more traditional and less desirable as judged by qualified independent observers. Consequently, the following related conclusions seem justified:

1. The possession of factual information about professional content does

not necessarily commit the teacher to actions consistent with that information.

2. Behavioral changes in prospective teachers can be more readily effected by programs of professional education which stress direct involvement of the prospective teacher in the teaching-learning process through meaningful laboratory experiences which are made relevant to content and theory.

3. Prospective teachers can be sensitized to the use of certain desirable teaching actions such as the use of praise and the acceptance of students' ideas through a planned professional program utilizing demonstration, observations and participation.

11. Sandefur, J.T. *Changing Teacher Behavior: A Description of Three Experimental Programs.* Paper presented at the annual meeting of the North Central Association of Colleges and Secondary Schools, March 1971, Chicago. 41 p., ED 049 168.

Three experimental programs were designed to examine whether the present content of teacher education affects the behavior of teachers in the classroom. The first study is described in detail in Item 10 above. The second study was primarily a follow-up to the first and examined the changes in teaching behavior exhibited during student teaching and during the last three weeks of the first year of teaching. The third study received only limited treatment because the final report had not yet been written. Findings of the second study included:

"The teachers (of the experimental group) became significantly more responsible, more understanding, more kindly, taught with more originality, were judged to be more attractive, more poised, more confident, more mature and integrated, and demonstrated more breadth in teaching."

Conclusions drawn from interaction analysis:

"(1) Teachers seem to reduce the percentage of time spent lecturing as a result of experience.

"(2) Experienced teachers tend to spend more time in directed practice than do inexperienced teachers.

"(3) The ratio of indirect verbal activity appears to increase with experience.

"(4) Extended direct influence appears to diminish as a result of experience.

"(5) Teachers sensitized in preservice professional programs to the use of indirect teacher influence, specifically to the acceptance of feeling, praise and encouragement and acceptance of students' ideas, seem to expand the use of these categories of directions, criticisms, and corrective feedback."

12. Shapiro, Bernard J. and Phyllis P. Shapiro. *The Relationship Between Satisfaction and Performance in Student Teaching* (1971). 14 p., ED 056 997.

The study explored the relationship between student teacher satisfaction with the classroom internship and the assessment of the student teacher's performance by the master teacher. Subjects were 50 college women randomly selected from seniors enrolled in the teacher education program of a four-year Catholic liberal arts college. Following the subjects' six-week experience in an elementary public school, each of the 50 master teachers was asked to rate her student teacher's overall classroom performance as either unsatisfactory, marginal, below average, above average, or outstanding.

" . . . there appears to be a close relationship between a student teacher's satisfaction with a student teaching experience and the evaluation of that student by the master teacher in whose class the student is working. This relationship, however, is not linear . . . those student teachers seen as either 'outstanding' or 'unsatisfactory' by their master teachers are the least satisfied, while higher levels of satisfaction are characteristic of student teachers in the 'average' ranges. Further, item analyses revealed that although the high performing and low performing student teachers are about equally dissatisfied with their student teaching experience, the basis for each group's dissatisfaction is not the same."

" . . . given the dissatisfaction of the 'outstanding' student teachers, will these students be lost to the profession? It is true that for the outstanding teacher, the dissonance of dissatisfaction may be perceived as an exciting challenge. It is also true that many of their difficulties seem related to their lack of independence in the master teacher's classroom, something which will not be a problem even in their first teaching position. Will they, however, remain in the profession until that first position?"

" . . . the responses to the satisfaction scale indicate that the student teaching experience is simply too standardized. Some of the students are ready for immediate classroom responsibility while others are not; some would be more at home in a child-centered classroom while others would find it easier to acclimatize in a subject-centered environment; some are anxious and ready to experiment with their own materials while others may initially need the security of a packaged lesson. Therefore, it would seem that individualized instruction needs to be brought to bear on teacher as well as on pupil education. The internship is central to professional preparation, but more resources must be devoted to its articulation and operation if it is to be adequate to the task. For example, (1) diagnostic procedures are necessary to assess both the readiness of the student teacher and the appropriateness of the 'match' with the master teachers, (2) college supervision needs to be a good deal more continuous and less desultory in order to assess the nature of the ongoing experience and make the appropriate adjustments, and (3) the length of the internship should be flexible so that students may remain apprentices until they are seen as ready for their first independent classroom assignment. Such changes may lead not only to great satisfaction but also in the long run to more adequate classroom performance."

13. Young, Dorothy A. and David B. Young. *The Effectiveness of Individually Prescribed Micro-Teaching Training Modules on an Intern's Subsequent Classroom Performance.* Paper presented at the annual meeting of the American Educational Research Association, February 1969, Los Angeles. 23 p., ED 030 586.

The effectiveness of individually prescribed micro-teaching modules in the acquisition of selected teaching behaviors was studied in two different contexts: during the pre-internship year in the MAT program at Johns Hopkins University and during student teaching in Teacher Education Centers at the University of Maryland. It was hypothesized that the experimental (micro-teaching) groups will (1) acquire a significantly greater number of selected, specific teaching behaviors, (2) have a significantly higher indirect-direct ratio, (3) acquire a greater number of alternative teaching patterns, and (4) make a significantly greater number of "emitted" responses. Findings support hypotheses (1) and (2).

"Results indicated that teacher candidates receiving individually prescribed micro-teaching training modules will acquire and implement a significantly greater number of specific teaching behaviors than candidates not receiving such training. The results also suggest that teachers trained in this manner will be more flexible and will exhibit alternative teaching patterns. These are preliminary findings and should in no way be considered conclusive."

14. Ziebarth, Raymond A. and Virginia C. Jones. *Secondary Education Individualized Instruction Project: A Curriculum/Instruction Study Project.* SEIIP Report No. 3., Omaha: University of Nebraska, August 1971. 77 p., ED 056 992.

The Secondary Education Individualized Instruction Project (SEIIP) is an attempt to place the preservice course on an individualized mode, using a systems-oriented, competency-based approach. During the summer session of 1970, the specification of course objectives and development of instructional packages was accomplished. The course material was divided into 12 units. The package for each unit contained the following elements: student directions, statement of objectives, assignment sheets, supplementary reading materials and criterion checks. The materials were field tested during the fall semester of the 1970-71 academic year. The major management and recordkeeping procedures were also developed during that period. During the spring semester of the same year, a study was conducted in which student achievement and attitudes under the individualized and traditional methods of instruction were compared. Specific objectives of the program were:

"(1) To develop a set of behaviorally stated objectives for competencies prospective teachers should display prior to student teaching.

"(2) To develop individualized instructional packets that will enable students to attain the objectives indicated in No. 1 above.

"(3) To explore ways of utilizing technology, media and alternate forms of class structuring to increase the behavioral changes desired in the prospective teachers.

"(4) To investigate ways in which to make better and more economical use of faculty and supporting staff.

"(5) To expose prospective teachers to newer developments and innovations in education as well as provide them with a better understanding of these developments."

"No significant difference was found between the two groups (experimental and control) in final achievement or in the amount of gain in achievement between the beginning and end of the course. Both groups made significant gains in achievement during the semester."

"In addition to the formal comparisons, a number of informal observations were made by the Instructional Staff concerning the attitude of students and other faculty toward the individualized instructional mode. This mode was a new experience for most students and many had strong reactions to the approach. Although much of the reaction tended to be positive, those who had negative attitudes toward the program were more extreme than those who were in the traditional mode of instruction. The students who successfully completed the course felt that the individualized instruction approach was worthwhile, although difficult at the onset. The new approach, which placed much responsibility on the student for achieving the learning outcomes, tended to discourage more students than did the traditional method of instruction. A larger percentage of Incompletes and Failures was noted in those classes in which the individualized instruction method was used. Those students who failed to complete the course tended to be students who were uncertain about their education goals or who appeared to have very little self-motivation and self-discipline."

The attitudes and reactions of students who experience the individualized instructional mode is more positive than that of students who are instructed by the more traditional means.

To be successful, the individualized instructional mode requires facilities, management, recordkeeping and staffing that are different from that needed to conduct a more traditional instructional operation.

15. Bradley, Ruth and others. *Measuring Teacher Competence: Research Backgrounds, Current Practice.* Burlingame: California Teachers Association, 1964. 47p., ED 040 152.

The many studies on teacher competence, usually biased toward specific viewpoints and concerned only with segments of the whole performance, demonstrate the need for a clearer definition. Methods used to determine effectiveness include measurement of pupil gains, job analysis and pupil ratings of teachers, all subject to inherent fallacies and limitations. The California Definition, published in 1952 by the California Teachers Association, has since been officially adopted by the state and identifies six teacher roles on the basis of the group or individuals with whom the teacher works. In 1950 the American Educational Research Association appointed a seven-member committee which established two general categories, relating directly to teacher effectiveness and to observable behavior and characteristics from which effectiveness may be inferred. In 1954 the American Psychological Association listed six categories: social validity, conceptualization, stability of the function, variability among the population, measurability, and ultimate-immediate relationships. The process of developing a measurement instrument is outlined, which provides enough flexibility to allow adaptation to local goals and philosophy.

16. Kay, Patricia M. and others. *Performance-Based Certification.* New York: University of New York, Office of Teacher Education, June 1971. 62 p., ED 056 991.

This annotated bibliography contains 115 citations ranging in date from 1957 to 1971. References are divided into five sections: (1) teacher certification and selection; (2) teacher education; (3) modeling, feedback and audio-visual media techniques; (4) observation, measurement and evaluation; and (5) research on teacher characteristics. When available, ERIC, author, American Educational Research Association, or other abstracts have been included with the citation.

17. American Association of Colleges for Teacher Education. *Performance-Based Teacher Education: An Annotated Bibliography.* Washington, D.C.: AACTE, 1971, 37 p., ED 050 034.

This 102-item annotated bibliography lists documents and journal articles published between 1967 and 1970. Citations are grouped under six categories. The first section lists documents describing the characteristics of actual or proposed programs of performance-based teacher education. The second section contains items related to certifying teachers on the basis of performance. The third section contains a selection from the literature on defining teacher competence. The basic elements of a performance-based curriculum are described in the fourth section, while the fifth deals with measuring the degree to which performance objectives are achieved and cites sources of information about specific assessment techniques. The sixth section lists documents indicating the attitude of teacher organizations toward performance assessment.